AP BIOLOGY REVIEW

PRACTICE QUESTIONS AND
ANSWER EXPLANATIONS

Island Prep Publishing

CONTENTS

INTRODUCTION

Advanced Placement Biology

Over the past decade, the number of students participating in the Advanced Placement Biology program has nearly doubled, with more than 200,000 students across the United States taking the exam in 2014. This trend is not unique to AP Biology. In recent years, student participation in the Advanced Placement program has increased in every subject across every demographic. Simply put, students are taking more AP exams in an effort to prepare for and gain admission to selective colleges. This book is designed to help relieve some of the pressure associated these high-stakes courses, and to provide students with the essential strategies, skills, and content to excel on the AP Biology exam.

The AP Biology course is for students who have an interest in the field of biology—a natural science concerned with the study of life and living organisms, including their structure, function, growth, evolution, distribution, and taxonomy. This course offers an opportunity for students interested in life sciences to earn Advanced Placement credit or exemption from a college-level biology course. Course topics include anatomy and physiology, biochemistry, biodiversity, cell functions and organelles, developmental biology, ecology, genetics, molecular biology, origin of life, population biology, evolution, molecular genetics, cell communication, and cell division. In addition to the standard biology topics above, students are required to be familiar with specific biology labs, as well as general lab procedure, which are covered in this review book. Finally, the AP Biology course requires students to engage in 7 broad scientific practices, including the use of representations and models to solve scientific problems; the use of mathematics; engagement in scientific questioning; planning and implementing data collection strategies; performing data analysis and evaluation of evidence; working with scientific explanations and theories; and connecting knowledge across domains.

The AP Biology exam contains 69 multiple-choice questions and 8 free-response questions. This book, which includes 550 practice questions with detailed explanations, will help students review the essential concepts, topics, and skills to master the AP Biology exam.

QUESTIONS

CHEMISTRY

LEVEL 1 DIFFICULTY

1. What type of attraction causes the double strand of DNA to stay together?

    (A) Chemical bonds
    (B) Hydrogen bonds
    (C) Van der waal forces
    (D) Adhesion
    (E) B and D

2. Hydrophobic properties are characteristic of all of the following except:

    (A) Equal electron distribution throughout the molecule
    (B) A long hydrocarbon chain
    (C) Soluble in water
    (D) None of the above

3. Hydrophillic literally means_____.

    (A) Water loving
    (B) Water fearing
    (C) Water soluble
    (D) Water insoluble

4. All of the following are proteins except:

    (A) Helicase
    (B) Lipase
    (C) Amylase
    (D) Lactose

5. All of the following are nucleic acids except:

   (A) DNA

   (B) M-RNA

   (C) T-RNA

   (D) ATP

   (E) Adenine

6. All of the following are types of carbohydrates except:

   (A) Starch

   (B) Glycogen

   (C) Glucose

   (D) Galactose

   (E) Histones

7. Which of the following occurs when a covalent bond is formed?

   (A) Electrons are shared.

   (B) The potential energy of the negative particles drop.

   (C) Electrons are transferred.

   (D) Metals and non-metals come together to achieve stability.

8. Which law of thermodynamics best explains why the potential energy within the bonds of glucose are conserved throughout cellular respiration?

   (A) The First Law of Thermodynamics

   (B) The Second Law of Thermodynamics

   (C) The Third law of Thermodynamics

   (D) None of the above

9. As PH increases basicity_____.

   (A) Increases

   (B) Decreases

   (C) Stays the same

LEVEL 2 DIFFICULTY

10. Which of the following types of molecules form a double layer and have both hydrophobic and hydrophilic components?

   (A) Helicase

   (B) Glucose

   (C) Pentose

   (D) Glycogen

   (E) Phospholipids

11. Refer to the below representation of a reaction:

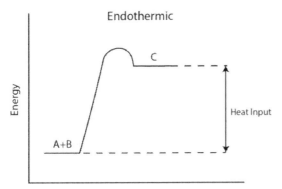

Which statement best describes this reaction pathway?

   (A) Exothermic, where the potential for a reaction to occur is greater in the products than the reactants.

   (B) Exothermic, where the potential for a reaction to occur is greater in the reactants than the products.

   (C) Endothermic, where the potential for a reaction to occur is greater in the products than the reactants.

   (D) Endothermic, where the potential for a reaction to occur is greater in the reactants than the products.

   (E) None of the above

Use the description of the flowing metabolic reaction to answer the next 5 consecutive questions:

In a series of metabolic reactions, substance A is converted into substance B by catalyst A', B' then catalyzes the production of substance C and then two products are then produced by the catalyst C_1', product D and product J. The production of D leads to the production of substance E by catalyst D'. C_1' also catalyzes the production of substance J and then J' catalyzes the production of substance K and then K' catalyzes the production of L.

12. Assuming that product E is an allosteric effector that inhibits enzyme C_1' if product E were not used in a subsequent reaction which of the following would most likely not occur?

   (A) The rate of production of substance D would decrease.

   (B) The rate of production of substance E would decrease.

   (C) The rate of production of substance L would decrease.

   (D) The rate of production of substance L would increase.

13. Assuming that product E is an allosteric effector that inhibits enzyme C_1', if product E were not used in a subsequent reaction which of the following would most likely occur?

   (A) The rate of production of substance D would decrease.

   (B) The rate of production of substance E would increase.

   (C) The rate of production of substance J would increase.

   (D) The rate of production of substance L would increase.

   (E) The rate of production of substance L will decrease.

   (F) Answers a and b

   (G) Answers a and e

14. The catalysts described in the metabolic reaction are most likely a(n)
_____.

(A) Nucleic acid

(B) Polypeptide

(C) Carbohydrate

(D) Phospholipid

(E) Enzyme

(F) Answers b and e

15. A', B', C₁', D', J' and K' are all examples of_____.

(A) Enzymes

(B) Polypeptides

(C) Molecules that have both hydrophobic and hydrophilic properties.

(D) Molecules that do not change throughout a chemical reaction.

(E) Answers a and b

(F) Answers a, b, and d

(G) All of the above

16. Substance L could be a(n)_____.

(A) Carbohydrate

(B) Protein

(C) Lipid

(D) All of the above

17. All of the following molecules are examples of polymers except:

(A) Protein

(B) Glucose

(C) Cellulose

(D) Starch

(E) Glycogen

18. All of the following are monomers except:

(A) Cytosine

(B) Amino acids

(C) Fructose

(D) Galactose

(E) Lactose

Note: Refer to the graph below for the next 3 consecutive questions

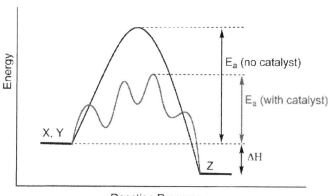

Reaction Progress

19. The red line describes the potential energy with a catalyst while the black line represents the potential energy within the system without an enzyme. Which statement does not apply to this graph?

(A) The red line could show the influence of an enzyme.

(B) The potential energy of Z is less than that of the summation of X and Y.

(C) This graph shows that the activation energy is lowered when a catalyst is introduced.

(D) The overall reaction is endergonic.

(E) None of the above

20. Which of the following statements best describes what happened to the potential energy throughout the reaction.

(A) Potential energy decreased throughout the reaction.

(B) Potential energy increased throughout the reaction.

(C) Potential energy remained the same throughout the reaction.

(D) What happened to the potential energy cannot be determined.

21. The potential energy of _____ equals delta G (note: delta means triangle and refers to the triangle G located on the graph).

(A) $x + y$

(B) $z - (x + y)$

(C) $(z - x) + y$

(D) $x - y + z$

(E) None of the above

Note: for the next 6 consecutive questions please refer to the following 5 molecules illustrated below.

(A)

(B)

(C)

(D)

(E)

22. Which of the above is a monosaccharide?_____

23. Which of the above contains a glyosidic linkage?_____

24. Which of the above is a polypeptide? _____

25. Which of the above is an amino acid? _____

26. Which of the above plays a major role in making up all membranes? _____

27. Which two of the above are examples of monomers? _____

28. A water molecule has two _____ and the over all molecule is _____.
    (A) nonpolar covalent bonds, nonpolar.
    (B) polar covalent bonds, nonpolar.
    (C) nonpolar covalent bonds, polar.
    (D) polar covalent bonds, polar.

29. Which of the following occurs when most covalent bonds form?
    (A) An unequal sharing of electrons.
    (B) Equal sharing of electrons.
    (C) One atom has all of the electrons.
    (D) The metal bonds to the non-metal.

30. Everything in nature tends toward_____ and _____.
    (A) Higher energy and greater stability.
    (B) Lower energy and greater stability.
    (C) Lower energy and less stability.
    (D) Higher energy and less stability.

31. If a reaction is endothermic then which of the following must be true?
    (A) The products have more potential energy than the reactants.
    (B) If the reverse reaction would be possible the reaction would be exothermic.
    (C) The reaction absorbs heat.
    (D) The reaction is considered uphill.
    (E) All of the above

32. When a molecule or atom is reduced it_____.
    (A) Loses potential energy.
    (B) Gains potential energy.
    (C) Does not change its potential energy.
    (D) None of the above

33. Which statement best describes the relationship between PH and hydrogen ion concentration?
    (A) As PH increases hydrogen ion concentration within a solution increases.
    (B) As PH increases hydrogen ion concentration within a solution decreases.
    (C) As PH decreases hydrogen ion concentration within a solution decreases.
    (D) As PH decreases hydrogen ion concentration within a solution increases.
    (E) Answers a and c
    (F) Answers b and d.

34. If a functional group within a molecule has a nitrogen with two hydrogens attached the molecule is most likely:
    (A) A polysaccharide
    (B) An enzyme
    (C) A weak base
    (D) A strong base
    (E) A phospholipid
    (F) Answers b and c
    (G) Answers b and d

35. Which best describes a polar molecule such as water?

(A) An electrically charged molecule where one end is positive and the other is negative.

(B) An electrically neutral molecule where, because of intramolecular interactions, a partial positive charge is generally associated with the location where hydrogen atoms are found, and a partial negative charge is found where oxygen atoms are found.

(C) An electrically neutral molecule where, because of intramolecular interactions, a partial negative charge is generally associated with the location where hydrogen atoms are found, and a partial positive charge is found where oxygen atoms are found.

(D) An electrically neutral atom where electron distribution is evenly distributed throughout the molecule.

(E) None of the above

36. Which statement best describes the relationship between galactose and lactose?

(A) Galactose is a monomer that serves as one of the two parts to lactose.

(B) Lactose is a monomer that serves as one of the two parts to galactose.

(C) Both Galactose and lactose are dimers of beta glucose.

(D) Both Galactose and lactose are dimers of alpha glucose.

(E) None of the above

37. Which of the following represents a catabolic reaction?

(A) $6H_2O + 6CO_2 + $ solar energy $\rightarrow C_6H_{12}O_6 + 6O_2$

(B) $2Mg + O_2 \rightarrow 2\,MgO$

(C) $CH_3CH_2CH_3 + H_2O \rightarrow CH_4 + CH_3CH_3$

(D) None of the above

Refer to the below representation of a reaction:

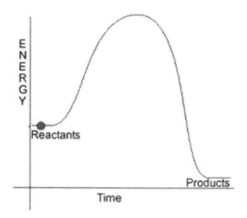

38. Which statement best describes this reaction pathway?

(A) Exothermic, where the potential for a reaction to occur is greater in the products than the reactants.

(B) Exothermic, where the potential for a reaction to occur is greater in the reactants than the products.

(C) Endothermic, where the potential for a reaction to occur is greater in the products than the reactants.

(D) Endothermic, where the potential for a reaction to occur is greater in the reactants than the products.

(E) None of the above

39. Which statement best describes the reason water is polar?

(A) Water dissociates into H+ and OH- ions and because of this the molecule is considered polar.

(B) Electrons spend more time near the hydrogen atoms due to its higher electronegativity, and therefore, it produces a net negative partial charge around the hydrogen atoms and a net positive partial charge near the oxygen atom.

(C) Electrons spend more time near the oxygen atom due its higher electronegativity, and therefore, it produces a net negative partial charge around the oxygen atom and a net positive partial charge near the hydrogen atoms.

(D) A difference in affinity for electrons between hydrogen and oxygen.

40. Some reactions occur spontaneously. Which statement best explains what this means and why this occurs?

(A) Some reactions occur in such a way that no energy is needed and the process is considered a down hill reaction. This occurs because everything tends toward greater stability, lower energy, and greater entropy.

(B) Some reactions occur in such a way that energy is needed and the process is considered a down hill reaction. This occurs because everything tends toward greater stability, lower energy, and greater entropy.

(C) Some reactions occur in such a way that no energy is needed and the process is considered a down hill reaction. This occurs because everything tends toward greater stability, lower energy, and less entropy.

(D) Some reactions occur in such a way that energy is needed and the process is considered a down hill reaction. This occurs because everything tends toward greater stability, lower energy, and less entropy.

41. Starch and glycogen play an important role within living things. Which statement best describes the relationship between starch and glycogen?

(A) Starch is found in plants while glycogen is found in animals. Both molecules are polymers of beta glucose.

(B) Starch is found in animals while glycogen is found in plants. Both molecules are polymers of beta glucose.

(C) Starch is found in plants while glycogen is found in animals. Both molecules are polymers of alpha glucose.

(D) Starch is found in animals while glycogen is found in plants. Both molecules are polymers of alpha glucose.

(E) None of the above

42. Which of the following explains why excess carbohydrates and excess fats within a biological organism readily convert into one another with relative ease?

(A) Fats and carbohydrates are ultimately made of the same types of atoms and rearranging their chemical bonds is what is necessary for converting fats to carbohydrates and visa versa.

(B) Fats and carbohydrates are both made from carbon hydrogen and Oxygen and the rearrangement of them is what determines their class of biological molecules.

(C) All of the above

Note: The following question refers to the diagram below:

43. All of the following are true except:

(A) Catabolic reactions break this molecule down into ADP + P_i.

(B) There is a large amount of potential energy associated with this molecule.

(C) This molecule is in the same class of biological molecules as DNA.

(D) The molecule can provide energy for doing work.

(E) This molecule is a monomer of the polymer that acts as an energy storage molecule.

17

CELL PARTS & PROCESSES

1. A prokaryotic cell has all of the following structures except:
   (A) Cytoplasm
   (B) Ribosomes
   (C) Nucleoid
   (D) Mitochondria

2. Which of the following are components of a plant cell wall?
   (A) Actin
   (B) Chitin
   (C) Cellulose
   (D) Helicase
   (E) Answer B and C

3. Which organelle's function is to break down waste products such as dead organelles in animal cells?
   (A) Lysosomes
   (B) Centrioles
   (C) The Golgi Body Apparatus
   (D) Ribosomes
   (E) None of the above

4. The receptor in plant cells that are sensitive to blue light are called _____.
   (A) Brassinolidines
   (B) Diacylglycerols
   (C) Rhodopsins
   (D) Cryptochromes
   (E) Phytochromes

5. If a virus were to attack a plant's cells that are primarily responsible for producing chemical energy which of the following is most likely the target cell structure that the virus attacked or inhibited?

    (A) Mitochondria

    (B) Nucleus

    (C) Chloroplast

    (D) Nucleolus

    (E) Endoplasmic reticulum

6. Which term best fits in the part of the diagram labeled "x"

Diagram:

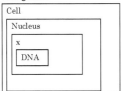

    (A) Nucleolus

    (B) Chromosome

    (C) Golgi body

    (D) Adenine

    (E) RNA

7. Choose the answer that best completes the sentence: The fluid mosaic model depicts _____ and_____ in a cross section for understanding the structure of_____.

    (A) Nucleic acids, carbohydrates, the nucleus

    (B) Phospholipids, carbohydrates, the cell membrane

    (C) Nucleic acids, carbohydrates, the cell membrane

    (D) Phospholipids, proteins, the cell membrane

8. The rough endoplasmic reticulum is absent in_____.

   (A) Higher plants

   (B) Streptococcus

   (C) Blue algae

   (D) Green algae

   (E) Answers C and D

9. Choose the answer that best fits the sentence: Some radio stations have had water-drinking contests that have led to the death of the contestants. These people consumed so much water that they had caused their *cells* to become _____ relative to the *outside environment*. In this circumstance your cells can _____, which ultimately causes death.

   (A) Hypotonic, expand and eventually burst

   (B) Hypotonic, shrink and eventually cause serious cell damage

   (C) Hypertonic, expand and eventually burst

   (D) Hypertonic, shrink and eventually cause serious cell damage

   (E) Isotonic, expand and eventually burst

10. Microtubules have all of the following characteristics except:

   (A) They function in cell division.

   (B) Their composition is that of a protein.

   (C) They are stored and organized in centrioles.

   (D) The rough endoplasmic reticulum (RER) synthesizes these structures.

Use the following choices for the next 7 consecutive questions:

(A) Osmosis

(E) Plasmolysis

(F) Bulk flow

(G) Active transport

(H) Facilitated diffusion

(I) Hypertonic

(J) Diffusion

11. Choose the answer above that best fits the following description: Net flow of water from an area of low solute concentration to an area of high concentration solutes through a semi-permeable membrane.

Answer: _____

12. Choose the answer above that best fits the following description: When a cell bursts due to it existing inside a hypotonic solution.

Answer: _____

13. Choose the answer above that best fits the following description: The net flow of large molecules from an area of 4 M of that large molecule to an area of 2 M of that molecule with the aid of proteins.

Answer: _____

14. Choose the answer above that best fits the following description: Blood moving throughout the circulatory system.

Answer: _____

15. Choose the answer above that best fits the following description: The net transfer of CO_2 from the circulatory system into the alveoli of the respiratory system.

Answer: _____

16. Choose the answer above that best fits the following description: The net movement of an essential nutrient molecule into a cell up its concentration gradient with the use of adenosine triphosphate.

Answer: _____

17. Choose the answer above that best fits the following description: Red blood cells tend to shrivel in this type of solution.

Answer: _____

18. Plant and animal cells differ in that _____.

(A) Plant cells do not have mitochondria.

(B) Only plant cells have flagella.

(C) Only animal cells have a phospholipid bilayer for a cell membrane.

(D) Only plant cells have a cell wall.

(E) Only plant cells have a vacuole.

(F) Answer D and E

19. If the enzyme catalase were some how inhibited within a peroxisome, what harmful chemical would accumulate?

(A) H_2O_2

(B) HCl

(C) Bile

(D) Lactic acid

20. The many functions of the smooth endoplasmic reticulum include all of the following except:

(A) The synthesis of lipids for replenishing dead or damaged membranes

(B) The synthesis of hormones

(C) The breakdown of toxins

(D) Assembling amino acids to make proteins

21. Sperm cells are much smaller in terms of volume when compared to female egg cells in humans. This is due to less _____.

(A) Mitochondria

(B) Golgi bodies

(C) Cytoplasm

(D) Genetic information

22. One mechanism that biological organisms use for ensuring that cells maximize their surface area to volume ratio is to develop cells that _____.

(A) Are short and fat.

(B) Have an oblate spheroid shape.

(C) Have long thin finger-like projections.

(D) Are able to optimize their cellular mobility while inhibiting their motility.

Refer to the following diagram for the next 4 consecutive questions:

Beaker 1   Beaker 2   Beaker 3

23. The cell inside beaker 1 is considered to be:

(A) In a hypotonic solution

(B) In a hypertonic solution

(C) In an Isotonic solution

(D) Answer A & B

(E) None of the above

24. Which beaker best represents the biological circumstance of an organism being dehydrated?

(A) Beaker 1

(B) Beaker 2

(C) Beaker 3

(D) None of the above beakers represents this circumstance.

25. Which beaker best represents the circumstance of a cell in a hypotonic solution and will cause all water molecules to move down its concentration gradient?

(A) Beaker 1

(B) Beaker 2

(C) Beaker 3

(D) None of the above beakers represents this circumstance.

26. Which beaker best represents the circumstance where a cell may burst?

(A) Beaker 1

(B) Beaker 2

(C) Beaker 3

(D) None of the above beakers represents this circumstance.

27. After a protein is assembled by a ribosome in the cytoplasm which organelle would it go to in order to become further modified?

(A) Mitochondria

(B) Lysosome

(C) Peroxisome

(D) Golgi body apparatus

(E) None of the above

28. Which of the following describes the reason why cells cannot be the size of a human?

(A) A cell needs to optimize its surface area to volume ratio in order to maximize its ability to both absorb nutrients and excrete wastes

(B) Increasing the volume of a cell puts a huge demand on the quantity of nutrients needed throughout the cell

(C) Cellular respiration rates would decrease

29. Differential centrifugation is a procedure that is ultimately:

(A) Used for separating "X" and "Y" sperm cells in order for potential parents to choose the sex of their progeny during in-vitro fertilization.

(B) Used for separating cells that may be different in terms of their density.

(C) Used for separating cell components.

(D) Answer A & B

(E) None of the above

30. If a toxin was to inhibit a cell's ribosomes, what cellular process would be most directly affected?

(A) Protein synthesis

(B) Cellular respiration

(C) DNA replication

(D) The degradation of cellular waste products

(E) None of the above

31. Which of the following best represents the correct sequence of events of a glycoprotein destined for secretion through the golgi complex?

(A) Cis face to medial region to trans face

(B) Trans face to cis face to medial region

(C) Trans face to medial region to cis face

(D) Cis face to trans face to medial region

(E) Medial region to trans face to cis face

32. Which cell structure plays an important role in apoptosis?

(A) Chloroplasts

(B) Nucleolus

(C) Peroxisomes

(D) Lysosomes

(E) Mitochondria

33. Choose the answer that best finishes the sentence: After using a procedure known as _____ you were able to isolate a cell structure. After analyzing it in the lab you were able to find that it is composed of alpha and beta tubulin. Based on the evidence the structure is most likely_____.

(A) Thin layer chromatography, a microfilament
(B) Differential centrifugation, a microfilament
(C) Thin layer chromatography, a microtubule
(D) Differential centrifugation, a microtubule

34. A doctor tells a man that he is infertile because his sperm cells lack the ability to swim. The organelle that is most directly affected in this case is the:

(A) Golgi body
(B) Cilia
(C) Nucleus
(D) Centrioles
(E) None of the above

35. Which of the following is not part of the endomembrane system?

(A) Vacuoles/Vesicles
(B) Smooth endoplasmic reticulum
(C) Golgi complex
(D) Peroxisomes
(E) None of the above

LEVEL 3 DIFFICULTY

36. If a person drinks enough water to make the solute concentration inside their red blood cells 2 Molar and the environment outside their red blood cells 2.1 Molar what will most likely occur?

(A) The cells will shrivel due to osmosis.
(B) The cells will shrivel due to active transport.
(C) The cells will expand due to osmosis.

(D) The cells will expand due to facilitated transport.

37. Which of the following include organelles that are involved in the endomembrane system?

(A) The nucleus

(B) The golgi body apparatus

(C) The smooth endoplasmic reticulum (SER)

(D) The rough endoplasmic reticulum (RER)

(E) Answer C & D

(F) Answer B, C, and D

38. Cell A is 10 micrometers in diameter, Cell B is 35 micrometers in diameter, Cell C is 45 micrometers in diameter and Cell D is 50 micrometers in diameter. Which of the following describes the correct order of how well each cell would absorb nutrients from *most* efficient to *least* efficient.

(A) Cell A, Cell B, Cell C, Cell D

(B) Cell D, Cell C, Cell B, Cell A

(C) None of the above

39. Throughout complex biological organisms there are structures that serve critical roles in maintaining homeostasis. These structures often have folds of some kind in order to _____.

(A) Absorb essential substances most efficiently
(B) Increase surface area of the structures
(C) Increase the surface area to volume ratio of the structure
(D) All of the above
(E) Answer A & B

40. It is considered to be an advantage for cells to be smaller because:

(A) A small cell will not weigh too much.
(B) A small cell occupies less space in nature where space is limited.
(C) A small cell has an immensely smaller volume relative to its surface area, which optimizes transport of essential material in and out of the cell.
(D) A small cell has an immensely smaller volume relative to its surface area, which promotes hydrogen ion balance between the inside and outside of cells.
(E) None of the above

41. Your task is to decipher the location of a specific protein within a cell using a colored stain. Which of the following is the best technique for this purpose?

(A) Electron microscopy
(B) Phase contrast microscopy
(C) Bright-field microscopy
(D) Fluorescence microscopy
(E) Dark-field microscopy

42. Electron microscopes have much higher capabilities in relation to viewing images than both light microscopes and the human eye because:

(A) Of their higher magnification.

(B) The lenses used are of much higher quality.

(C) Of the very short (nanometer) wavelengths of electrons.

(D) The images are viewed on screens rather than directly through an eye piece or by the naked eye.

(E) All of the above

43. A single cell in a person's epithelial squamous tissue becomes cancerous. It doubles its DNA and divides much faster than other neighboring cells. The location of the change that occurred in this cell most likely originated in the _____.

(A) Mitochondria

(B) Nucleus

(C) Nucleolus

(D) Ribosome

(E) Answer B & C

(F) None of the above

CELLULAR RESPIRATION

1. What is the primary advantage to alcoholic fermentation as it relates to cellular respiration?

   (A) It produces ATP

   (B) It uses oxidative phosphorylation in order to produce ATP

   (C) It replenishes NAD+ so that substrate level phosphorylation in the cytoplasm can occur there by netting 2 molecules of ATP

   (D) It replenishes CO_2 for the dark reactions.

   (E) None of the above

Refer to the diagram below this description to answer the next 10 consecutive questions. The three circles represent the three consecutive major events in aerobic respiration.

2. Which of the above pathways exist only inside the mitochondria?

   (A) Pathway 1

   (B) Pathway 2

   (C) Pathway 3

   (D) Answer b &c

   (E) All of the above

3. All of the above pathways produce CO_2 except

   (A) Pathway 1

   (B) Pathway 2

(C) Pathway 3

(D) All of the above produce CO_2

(E) None of the above produce CO_2

4. Which of the following best match the description of pyruvate?

(A) A 3 carbon chain made as a product from pathway 1 and used as a reactant for pathway 2

(B) A 3 carbon chain made as a product from pathway 1 and used as a reactant for pathway 3

(C) A necessary molecule for the overall reaction to enter into the mitochondria

(D) Answer b &c

(E) None of the above

5. Which of the above pathways use oxidative phosphorylation in order to produce ATP?

(A) Pathway 1

(B) Pathway 2

(C) Pathway 3

(D) Answer a &b

(E) None of the above

6. Which of the above reactions use NADPH in order to help synthesize ATP?

(A) Pathway 1

(B) Pathway 2

(C) Pathway 3

(D) Answer a &b

(E) None of the above

7. Which of the choices below best describe substrate level phosphorylation?

(A) It occurs in pathway 1

(B) It occurs in pathway 2

(C) It produces a net of 2 molecules of ATP

(D) All of the above

(E)   None of the above

8.   Pathway 3 is called the
   (A)   Krebs cycle
   (B)   Glycolysis
   (C)   Electron transport chain
   (D)   Calvin cycle
   (E)   None of the above

9.   Which of the above reaction pathways yield the most ATP?
   (A)   Pathway 1
   (B)   Pathway 2
   (C)   Pathway 3

10.   The reactants to pathway 3 are
   (A)   ADP, O_2 NAD+, $FADH_2$
   (B)   ADP, CO_2, NADH, $FADH_2$
   (C)   Glucose and oxygen
   (D)   Pyruvate and ADP
   (E)   None of the above

11.   What are the reactants to pathway 2?
   (A)   NADH
   (B)   ADP
   (C)   Pyruvate
   (D)   Answer b & c
   (E)   All of the above

12.   What are the products of pathway 3?
   (A)   ATP and H_2O
   (B)   ATP and CO_2
   (C)   ATP and $FADH_2$
   (D)   None of the above

13. Choose the answer that best finishes the sentence: Without _____ the over all respiration reaction will continue in the cytoplasm and produce less ATP.

    (A) O_2

    (B) H_2O

    (C) Glucose

    (D) $FADH_2$

    (E) None of the above

14. What is the primary role of oxygen in aerobic respiration?

    (A) Oxygen is used to split glucose into two 3-carbon molecules

    (B) Oxygen donates its electrons at the end of the electron transport chain

    (C) Oxygen accepts electrons at the end of the electron transport chain

    (D) Oxygen is necessary to carry the waste product carbon dioxide away

    (E) None of the above

15. Which of the following occurs during anaerobic respiration

    (A) The krebs cycle

    (B) Oxidative phosphorylation

    (C) The conversion of pyruvate to ethanol

    (D) The electron transport chain

    (E) None of the above

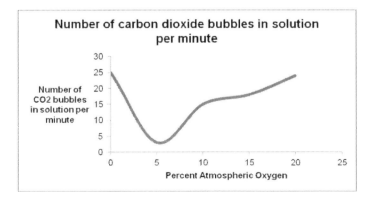

The figure above depicts data that was collected from a student who exposed a sample of animal cells to varying percent atmospheric oxygen. Refer to this graph when answering the next 2 consecutive questions.

16. At levels below 2 % the number of CO_2 bubbles released relative to the rest of the y-axis data set is high. This is most probably because
    (A) There are excess hydroxide ions
    (B) There are excess hydrogen ions
    (C) The temperature has been manipulated
    (D) Lactic acid fermentation is occurring
    (E) None of the above

17. Krebs cycle activity most likely starts increasing at
    (A) 0 % atmospheric oxygen
    (B) 5 % atmospheric oxygen
    (C) 10 % atmospheric oxygen
    (D) 15 % atmospheric oxygen
    (E) None of the above

18. Someone who lacks athletic activity on a daily basis will probably have excess
    (A) Lactic acid
    (B) Glycogen
    (C) Lipidogenesis reactions
    (D) CO_2
    (E) Answer b & c
    (F) All of the above

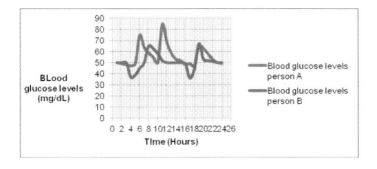

Base the next 4 consecutive questions on the graph illustrated above.

19. Choose the answer that best completes the sentence: Person A most likely
    has higher _____ than person B in respective muscle tissue.

    (A) Average P_i concentration through out tissue

    (B) Average CO_2 concentration through out tissue

    (C) Average ADP concentration through out tissue

    (D) Average ATP concentration through out tissue

    (E) None of the above

20. Choose the answer that best fits completes the sentence. A valid conclusion that someone could come to is that person A was _____ than person B and Person B probably _____.

   (A) Less active, worked out once through out the day
   (B) Less active, worked out twice throughout the day
   (C) More active, ate 3 meals throughout the day
   (D) More active, ate 3 meals throughout the day.

21. The rate of Krebs cycle activity was probably highest in

   (A) Person A between 10 and 11 hours
   (B) Person A between 4 and 6 hours
   (C) Person B between 15 and 17 hours
   (D) Person B between 2 and 4 hours
   (E) None of the above

22. Which statement (s) is/ are valid?

   (A) Person A had 3 square meals through out the day and his body effectively brought his blood glucose level back to equilibrium
   (B) Person B will have a larger buildup of lactic acid through out the day than person B
   (C) Person A most likely engaged in exercise through out the day
   (D) Person A never works out
   (E) Answer a & b
   (F) None of the above

23. The term Glycolysis refers to:

   (A) The splitting of a 6 carbons ring into two 3-carbon chained molecules
   (B) Generating 2 molecules of ATP through a series of reactions that occur inside the mitochondria
   (C) The use of a proton gradient to generate the energy needed to phosphorylate ADP into ATP
   (D) Light independent reactions
   (E) None of the above

24. The Krebs cycle is
   (A) A process that occurs inside the mitochondria
   (B) A process that generates ATP
   (C) A process that occurs as a second step relative to the three major steps of cellular respiration
   (D) A process that generates CO_2
   (E) All of the above

Use the following terms as an answer bank for the following 10 questions

   (A) Glycolysis
   (F) Cell membrane
   (G) Oxidative phosphorylation
   (H) Thylakoid
   (I) Lumen
   (J) Alcoholic fermentation
   (K) Lactic acid fermentation
   (L) Substrate level phosphorylation
   (M) Krebs cycle
   (N) Electron transport chain
   (O) ADP synthase
   (P) Cristae matrix
   (Q) ATP synthase
   (R) Hydrogen Ion gradient
   (S) Electron gradient

25. A _____ is created in order to generate ADP into ATP during the electron transport chain

26. _____ is a reaction that exists in cellular respiration that generates two molecules of ATP and two 3 carbon molecules by splitting glucose in the cytoplasm of a cell.

27. _____ is a reaction that occurs in animals without the presence of O_2.

28. _____ is a protein that moves like a machine and uses the potential energy from H+ to phosphorylate ADP into ATP.

29. Single celled prokaryotic organisms are able to generate energy through the process of_____.

30. _____ is the process that generates ATP from ADP during Glycolysis and the Krebs Cycle.

31. _____ is the location of a PH gradient that exists to aid in the production of the most efficient amount of ATP relative to the other two major processes that exist in aerobic respiration.

32. _____ is the process that generates ATP from ADP when a voltage gradient is produced.

33. _____ is the step in cellular respiration that produces 34 molecules of ATP.

34. _____ is a set of reactions that occurs inside the mitochondria and produces CO_2.

Refer to the chart below when answering the next 8 consecutive questions

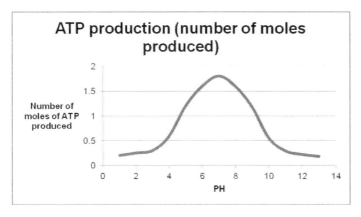

The above illustrates a series of respiration reactions inside a students test tube.

35. A valid conclusion based on the above data could be that

(A) ATP is produced most efficiently at neutral PH's

(B) ATP is produced most efficiently when H+ and OH- are in a 1:1 ratio

(C) ATP is produced most efficiently at an acidic PH

(D) ATP is produced most efficiently at a basic PH

(E) Answer a &b

36. A PH of _____ portrays optimum ATP production.

(A) 1

(B) 13

(C) 7

(D) None of the above

37. Assuming the % yield of products during this set of respiration reactions were 99.9% during the most optimum PH, about how many moles of glucose was initially used for these reactions if the reaction were to have continued into the mitochondria?

(A) .01

(B) .05

(C) .03

(D) .02

(E) Cannot be determined

38. If these reactions continued into the mitochondria these reactions most likely occurred inside a(n)

(A) Plant cell

(B) Animal cell

(C) Prokaryotic cell

(D) Cannot be determined

(E) Answer a or b

39. Which of the following solvents would yield the most ATP according to the above data?

(A) H_2O

(B) CH_3CH_2OH

(C) HCl

(D) NaOH

(E) None of the above

40. If the reactions continued into the mitochondria these reactions most likely occurred

(A) Through the process of alcoholic fermentation

(B) Through the process of lactic acid fermentation

(C) Through the process of anaerobic respiration

(D) Through the process of aerobic respiration

(E) Cannot be determined based on the above data

41. High H+ concentration yields

    (A) Low quantities of ATP

    (B) High quantities of ATP

    (C) High molar quantities of chemical energy

    (D) None of the above

42. High OH- concentration yields

    (A) Low quantities of ATP

    (B) High quantities of ATP

    (C) High molar quantities of chemical energy

    (D) None of the above

LEVEL 3 DIFFICULTY

43. Chemiosmosis is a concept that explains how ATP is synthesized from ADP. Which of the following explains how ATP is ultimately generated from ADP?

    (A) Electrons flowing through ATP Synthase generate the energy necessary to synthesize ATP from ADP.

    (B) A PH gradient is generated which provides the energy needed in order to phosphorylate ADP into ATP

    (C) The Krebs Cycle generates an electron gradient between the inner and the outer membrane which generates a proton gradient which generates the energy to phosphorylate ADP into ATP.

    (D) Glycolysis generates an electron gradient between the inner and the outer membrane which generates a proton gradient which generates the energy to phosphorylate ADP into ATP.

    (E) None of the above

PHOTOSYNTHESIS

1. What is the original source of free energy that all organisms use either directly or indirectly?
   (A) Solar energy
   (B) Plant life
   (C) Phosphorylation reactions
   (D) Gravity
   (E) Acids

2. Chlorophyll is found in
   (A) Thylakoid membranes
   (B) Stroma
   (C) Lumen
   (D) Guard cells
   (E) None of the above

3. P700 and P680 are
   (A) Both identical chlorophyll-a molecules
   (B) Pigment molecules that interact with different proteins within the thylakoid membranes
   (C) Have different electron distributions
   (D) Answer b &c
   (E) All of the above

4. In the fall the colors of deciduous trees change from green to reds, oranges, and yellows. This is due to which of the following?

    (A) Chlorophyll a
    (B) Chlorophyll b
    (C) Carotenoids
    (D) Degradation of H_2O_2 into water
    (E) Answer a & b

5. Noncyclic photophosphorylation produces

    (A) NADH
    (B) NAD+
    (C) NADP+
    (D) NADPH
    (E) ATP
    (F) CO_2

6. Which of the following molecules contains the least stored energy?

    (A) ADP
    (B) ATP
    (C) NADPH
    (D) Glucose
    (E) Starch

7. Which of the following best explains why non-cyclic photophosphorylation is indeed non-cyclic?

    (A) The electrons are not recycled and they are used to aid in the production of NADH
    (B) The electrons are not recycled and they are used to aid in the production of NADPH
    (C) ATP molecules are not recycled and they are used to aid in the production of NADH

(D) ATP molecules are not recycled and they are used to aid in the production of NADPH

(E) None of the above.

8. Which of the following best explains why cyclic photophosphorylation is indeed cyclic

(A) Electrons move in a cyclic manor and it aids in the production of NADPH

(B) Electrons move in a cyclic manor and it aids in the production of ATP

(C) Protons move in a cyclic manor and it aids in the production of NADPH

(D) Protons move in a cyclic manor and it aids in the production of ATP

(E) None of the above

Use the following 7 choices to answer the next 7 consecutive questions.

(A) Outer membrane

(F) Inner membrane

(G) Intermembrane space

(H) Stroma

(I) Thylakoids

(J) Granum

(K) Thylakoid lumen

9. The membrane that consists of a double layer membrane of phospholipids, which separates the chloroplast from its outside environment, is called ____.

10. The narrow space between the inner and the outer membrane is called the _____.

11. A second double layer membrane in the chloroplast is called the _____.

12. Fluid material that fills the inside of the inner membrane. The Calvin cycle occurs here in the _____.

13. Pancake like membranes inside the chloroplast that contain photosystems II, I, cytochromes, and other electron carriers of the light dependent reactions. _____

14. Stacks of thylakoid membranes are called_____.

15. The inside of a thylakoid membrane where H+ ions accumulate are called _____ .

Base the following question on the graph below where a student observed a series of respiration reactions from animal tissue in solution.

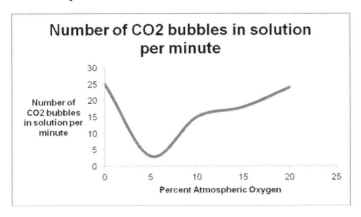

16. Which of the following statements describes why this graph does not describe photosynthesis?

   (A) CO_2 levels eventually increase which is not characteristic of photosynthesis

   (B) CO_2 Levels increase directly after reaction starts

   (C) The control shows that there is a relatively high CO_2 amount being produced

   (D) CO_2 levels from 0-5 indicate that CO_2 is being used

   (E) None of the above

For the next 3 consecutive questions refer to the graph below

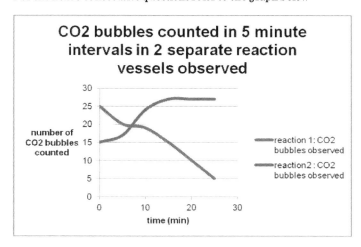

17. Reaction 1 is most likely

   (A) Photosynthesis

   (B) An oxidative phosphorylation reaction

   (C) Light reactions

   (D) Answer a & c

   (E) All of the above

18. Reaction 2 is most likely

   (A) Photosynthesis

   (B) A series of Kreb cycle reactions

   (C) A series of Calvin cycle reactions

   (D) None of the above

19. The relationship that most likely exists between reaction 1 and 2 is that

   (A) Reaction 1 most likely exists in plants while reaction 2 most likely exists in animals

   (B) Reaction 1 most likely exists in animals while reaction 2 most likely exists in plants

(C) They could be opposite reactions

(D) Reaction 1 uses CO_2 while reaction 2 produces CO_2

(E) Answers c &d

(F) All but b

(G) All but a

20. Cyclic photophosphorylation

(A) Combines O_2 with RuBP

(B) Has electrons that move along an electron transport chain

(C) Stores energy obtained from light into NADPH

(D) Is a metabolic pathway that involves the transfer of substances between two types of cells

(E) Occurs in the stroma of the chloroplast

(F) Requires electrons that are obtained by splitting water

(G) Answer c &f

21. Non- Cyclic photophosphorylation

(A) Combines O_2 with RuBP

(B) Has electrons that move along an electron transport chain

(C) Stores energy obtained from light into NADPH

(D) Is a metabolic pathway that involves the transfer of substances between two types of cells

(E) Occurs in the stroma of the chloroplast

(F) Requires electrons that are obtained by splitting water

(G) Answer c &f

22. Photorespiration

(A) Combines O_2 with RuBP

(B) Has electrons that move along an electron transport chain

(C) Stores energy obtained from light into NADPH

(D) Is a metabolic pathway that involves the transfer of substances between two types of cells

(E) Occurs in the stroma of the chloroplast

(F) Requires electrons that are obtained by splitting water

23. The Calvin cycle
    (A) Combines O_2 with RuBP
    (B) Has electrons that move along an electron transport chain
    (C) Stores energy obtained from light into NADPH
    (D) Is a metabolic pathway that involves the transfer of substances between two types of cells
    (E) Occurs in the stroma of the chloroplast
    (F) Requires electrons that are obtained by splitting water
    (G) Answer c &f

24. C_4 Photosynthesis
    (A) Combines O_2 with RuBP
    (B) Has electrons that move along an electron transport chain
    (C) Stores energy obtained from light into NADPH
    (D) Is a metabolic pathway that involves the transfer of substances between two types of cells
    (E) Occurs in the stroma of the chloroplast
    (F) Requires electrons that are obtained by splitting water
    (G) Answer c &f

25. Which series of reactions produces glucose?
    (A) Noncyclic photophosphorylation
    (B) Cyclic photophosphorylation
    (C) Electron transport chain
    (D) Calvin cycle
    (E) None of the above

Refer to the following diagram to answer the next 5 consecutive questions

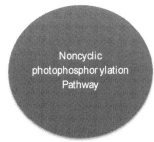 

26. Choose the best answer: What are the reactants for noncyclic photophosphorylation?

    (A) Water, solar energy, NADPH, ADP
    (B) Water, solar energy, NADP+, ADP
    (C) Glucose, ATP, CO_2, solar energy
    (D) Glucose, ADP, CO_2, Solar energy
    (E) None of the above

27. Choose the best answer: What are the products for noncyclic photophosphorylation?

    (A) ATP, NADPH, O_2
    (B) ADP, NADP+, O_2
    (C) Glucose, NADP+, ADP
    (D) Glucose, NADPH, ADP

28. What does noncyclic photophosphorylation produce that is then used in the calvin cycle?

    (A) ATP
    (B) NADP+
    (C) NADPH
    (D) O_2
    (E) Answer a & c
    (F) All but answer b

29. Which of the following products of the Calvin cycle does not get recycled through photosynthesis?

(A) ADP

(B) ATP

(C) Glucose

(D) NADP+

(E) None of the above

30. Which of the following is used by the Calvin cycle but not produced by noncyclic photophosphorylation?

(A) NADP+

(B) NADPH

(C) CO_2

(D) ATP

(E) Answer b & c

31. Which of the following statements about photosynthesis is false?

(A) NADPH is produced during noncyclic photophosphorylation

(B) The Calvin cycle occurs at night

(C) A PH gradient drives the formation of ATP from ADP

(D) Carbon dioxide is used through out the photosynthetic process

(E) None of the above

32. PEP carboxylase is

(A) An enzyme that combines with CO_2 in C_3 photosynthesis

(B) An enzyme that combines with CO_2 in C_4 photosynthesis

(C) An enzyme that combines with CO_2 to produce OAA in CAM photosynthesis

(D) Answer b & c

(E) All of the above

Refer to the following diagram to answer this question:

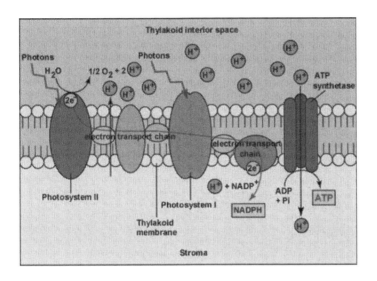

33. Which of the following is true of the above diagram?

    (A) A PH gradient is present

    (B) A voltage gradient is present

    (C) An electrochemical gradient is necessary to turn the ATP synthase pump in order to phosphorylate ATP from ADP

    (D) Hydrogen ions are able to pass through the ATP synthase protein but not the thylakoid membrane

    (E) All of the above

34. Which of the following is evidence that chloroplasts were single celled organisms that were engulfed by bigger cells?

    (A) They have their own DNA

    (B) They have rough endoplasmic reticulum

    (C) They have thylakoids

    (D) All of the above

35. What is the significance of P700 as it relates to photosynthesis?

    (A) It functions during the Krebs cycle

(B) It absorbs light at 700 nanometers during photosystem II

(C) It functions during the carbon fixation reactions

(D) It functions during photosystem I

(E) Answer d &b

(F) None of the above

36. What is the significance of P680 as it relates to photosynthesis?

(A) It functions during the Krebs cycle

(B) It absorbs light at 680 nanometers during photosystem II

(C) It functions during the carbon fixation reactions

(D) It functions during photosystem I

(E) Answer d &b

(F) None of the above

37. Photorespiration is a process that is

(A) Efficient because it fixes only CO_2

(B) Not efficient because instead of fixing CO_2 alone it also fixes some O_2

(C) Not efficient because combining RuBP with O_2 does not produce molecules with relatively high levels of potential energy

(D) Efficient because combining RuBP with O_2 produces molecules with relatively high levels of potential energy

(E) Answer a and d

(F) Answer b and c

38. Peroxisomes function in photosynthesis by

(A) Breaking down photorespiration products

(B) Aiding in the PH gradient produced during the electron transport chain by secreting more electrons

(C) Aiding in the PH gradient produced during the electron transport chain by secreting more H+ ions

(D) Aiding in the absorption of p700

(E) None of the above

39. CO_2 is moved to bundle sheath cells in

(A) C_3 photosynthesis

(B) C_4 photosynthesis

(C) CAM photosynthesis

(D) All of the above

(E) None of the above

40. CAM photosynthesis is identical to C_4 photosynthesis in all of the following ways except in CAM photosynthesis:

(A) PEP carboxylases fix CO_2

(B) OAA is converted into Malic acid

(C) CO_2 is converted into OAA

(D) Answer a and c

(E) None of the above

41. Which of the following does not occur in noncyclic photophosphorylation
    (A) Electrons are energized by light
    (B) Electrons are trapped by P_{680}
    (C) NADPH is produced
    (D) Energized electrons from PSI join with protein carriers and generate ATP as they pass along the electron transport chain
    (E) Chemical energy is produced in the form of ATP

42. CAM photosynthesis and C_4 Photosynthesis are very similar photosynthetic pathways. One way that they differ is that CAM photosynthetic pathways
    (A) Fixes CO_2 by rubisco into PGA
    (B) Converts CO_2 into OAA by combining with PEP carboxylase
    (C) At night stomata are open, PEP carboxylase is active, and malic acid accumulates in the cells vacuoles
    (D) Malate does not get transferred from mesophyll cells to bundle sheath cells
    (E) Answer c & d
    (F) Answer a & b
    (G) None of the above

43. What is the relationship between the overall reactions of photosynthesis and cellular respiration?
    (A) They are the same with the exception that instead of light energy used in photosynthesis, food energy is used for cellular respiration
    (B) They are the same with the exception that instead of light energy used in photosynthesis, food energy is used for cellular respiration
    (C) They are opposite reactions where food energy is produced in cellular respiration and chemical energy is produced during photosynthesis
    (D) They are opposite reactions where chemical energy is produced in cellular respiration and food energy is produced during photosynthesis
    (E) None of the above

CELL DIVISION

LEVEL 1 DIFFICULTY

1. At what point does DNA get copied in the cell cycle?
   (A) G1-phase
   (B) G2-phase
   (C) S-phase
   (D) M-phase
   (E) None of the above

2. All of the following is considered to be part of the interphase portion of the cell cycle except:
   (A) G1-phase
   (B) G2-phase
   (C) S-phase
   (D) M-phase

3. All of the following is true except:
   (A) Humans have 46 chromosomes
   (B) Males have one Y chromosome
   (C) Some plant cells contain centrioles
   (D) Gap 1 phase is essentially a growth phase for a cell

4. A centromere is
   (A) A structure that is made of the protein histone
   (B) A structure that is made of the protein kinetochore
   (C) A structure that holds sister chromatids in an X like shape known as chromosomes
   (D) Answer a &c
   (E) Answer b & c

5. DNA replication is regulated and maintained most directly by the
   _____ checkpoint.

   (A) G1- phase
   (B) G2-phase
   (C) Metaphase
   (D) M- phase

6. Microtubules primarily make up which of the following structures?

   (A) Nuclear envelope
   (B) Chromosomes
   (C) Centrioles
   (D) DNA
   (E) None of the above

7. Genetic variation is an advantage caused by which type of cell division?

   (A) Budding
   (B) Regeneration
   (C) Mitosis
   (D) Meiosis
   (E) None of the above

LEVEL 2 DIFFICULTY

8. What is the key difference between chromatin and a chromatid?

   (A) Chromatin is a single copy of a duplicated chromosome and a chromatid
   is uncondensed DNA.
   (B) Corresponding maternal and paternal chromatids are identical in all
   aspects with the exception that they carry different alleles while a
   chromatin is a set of two of these
   (C) Chromatin is uncondensed DNA while chromatids are a single copy of a
   duplicated chromosome.
   (D) None of the above

9. At what point in the cell cycle does the cell only mature or grow?

    (A) G1-phase
    (B) G2-phase
    (C) S-phase
    (D) M-phase
    (E) Answer a & b
    (F) None of the above

10. Check points to be sure the genetic material has been synthesized and maintained in the correct sequence exits after:

    (A) G1-phase
    (B) G2-phase
    (C) S-phase
    (D) M-phase
    (E) All but answer d is correct
    (F) All but answer c is correct

11. Which of the following phases of the cell cycle ensures a copy of DNA will be present for a new cell that is made after cell division has taken place?

    (A) G1-phase
    (B) G2-phase
    (C) S-phase
    (D) M-phase
    (E) All of the above

12. Which of the following phases does the genetic material exist as chromosomes?

    (A) G1-phase
    (B) G2-phase
    (C) S-phase
    (D) M-phase
    (E) Answer a &b

13. If a cell is born with x amount of DNA, in what phase does the amount of DNA become 2x?

   (A) G1-phase
   (B) G2-phase
   (C) S-phase
   (D) M-phase
   (E) Answer a &b

14. Each human somatic cell contains

   (A) 23 sets of 2 homologous chromosomes
   (B) 46 chromosomes
   (C) 92 sister chromatids
   (D) One X chromosome in the 23rd set of chromosomes
   (E) All of the above

Refer to a mitotically dividing cell and the lettered choices provided for the next 10 consecutive questions. Answers can be used once, multiple times, or not at all.

   (A) Telophase
   (F) Anaphase
   (G) Prophase
   (H) Metaphase
   (I) interphase

15. This is the phase of the cell cycle where chromatin starts to organize into chromosomes. _____

16. This is the phase of the cell cycle where chromosomes line up one underneath the other on the mitotic plate. _____

17. This is the phase of the cell cycle where chromosomes are separated into their respective sister chromatids and the spindle fibers pull these toward opposite poles of the cell. _____

18. This is the phase of the cell cycle where the cytoplasm pinches and two new cells form. _____

19. This is the phase of the cell cycle where the nuclear envelope starts to reappear. ____

20. This is the phase of the cell cycle where centrioles start moving to the opposite poles. _____

21. This is the phase the cell cycle where the genetic material is organized as chromatin. _____

22. This is the phase of the cell cycle where the cell grows and matures. _____

23. This is the phase of the cell cycle where the cell's DNA is copied. _____

24. In the early stages of this phase of the cell cycle there are two nuclei present in the cell. _____

Refer to the following diagram of a mitotically dividing cell to answer the following 2 questions:

25. What phase of mitosis is this cell in?

    (A) prophase

    (B) interphase

    (C) anaphase

    (D) metaphase

    (E) telophase

26. What is the ploidy of this cell?

    (A) 2n=3

    (B) n=3

    (C) 3n=2

    (D) 2n=6

    (E) n=6

27. In what type of cell division does the event crossing over occur?

    (A) Spermatogenesis

    (B) Meiosis

    (C) Mitosis

    (D) Asexual reproduction

    (E) Answer a &b

    (F) Answer c & d

28. Crossing over occurs in

    (A) Prophase I

    (B) Prophase

    (C) Metaphase I

    (D) Metaphase

    (E) None of the above

Refer to the following lettered answers to answer the next 10 questions. Answers can be used once, multiple times, or not at all.

    (A) diploid

    (F) haploid

    (G) triploid

    (H) 2n=46

    (I) n=22

    (J) 2n=45

    (K) n=23

    (L) Trisomy 21

    (M) Huntington's disease

    (N) Meiosis I

    (O) Meiosis II

    (P) Mitosis

29. Any organism that has a male and a female parent. _____

30. Having one set of DNA because of having only one parent. _____

31. Is a type of cell division that is associated with asexual reproduction. _____

32. Occurs when non disjunction event occurs. _____

33. Another name for down syndrome. _____

34. Humans have this ploidy in their autosomes. ____

35. Humans have this ploidy in their sex cells. _____

36. Humans have this ploidy in their somatic cells. _____

37. Humans have this ploidy in their gametes. _____

38. This part of sexual reproduction of cells is the origin of genetic variation via crossing over. _____

39. If the normal number of chromosomes in a cell is 12 how many chromosomes will be present after meiosis has taken place?

(A) 12

(B) 6

(C) 3

(D) 24

(E) none of the above

40. A non-disjunction event occurs on the first chromosome set in a human. This human will most likely:

(A) Die

(B) Have Huntington's disease

(C) Have down syndrome

(D) Have sickle celled anemia

(E) None of the above

41. A cell has 50 chromosomes at the beginning of meiosis how many chromosomes are in each cell in anaphase II?

   (A) 50
   (B) 100
   (C) 25
   (D) 10

42. f a somatic cell of an animal is 2n= 32 then its corresponding gametes will have a ploidy of_____.

   (A) 2n=32
   (B) n=32
   (C) n=16
   (D) 4n=32

43. The following are illustrations of cells with chromosomes. Each shape represents a different chromosome. Which cell represents a cell that has a ploidy of 2n=6?

   (A)   (B)

   (C)   (D)

44. How many chromatids are present in a cell after meiosis I has taken place in an organism where the normal ploidy of the somatic cells of that organism is 2n=16?

(A) 8
(B) 16
(C) 32
(D) 1
(E) cannot be determined based on the information given

HEREDITY

LEVEL 1 DIFFICULTY

1. Which best describes the concept of an allele
   (A) Genes for eye color and hair length
   (B) Genes for green eyes and long hair
   (C) Genes for green eyes and brown eyes
   (D) Genes for wrinkled and yellow peas
   (E) None of the above

2. A human genetic defect that is caused by autosomal non disjunction is
   (A) Turner syndrome
   (B) Down syndrome
   (C) Sickle celled anemia
   (D) Hemophilia
   (E) Red green colorblindness

3. Huntington's disease is a(n)
   (A) Autosomal recessive disorder
   (B) Autosomal dominant disorder
   (C) X-linked dominant disorder
   (D) X-linked recessive disorder
   (E) Y-linked disorder

4. Hemophilia is a(n)
   (A) Autosomal recessive disorder
   (B) Autosomal dominant disorder
   (C) X-linked dominant disorder
   (D) X-linked recessive disorder
   (E) Y-linked disorder

5. Red-green color blindness in a(n)

   (A) Autosomal recessive disorder
   (B) Autosomal dominant disorder
   (C) X-linked dominant disorder
   (D) X-linked recessive disorder
   (E) Y-linked disorder

LEVEL 2 DIFFICULTY

6. If you roll a pair of 12-sided dice what is the probability that both dice will turn up as a five?

   $$\frac{1}{12} \cdot \frac{1}{12}$$

   (A) 1/4
   (B) 1/8
   (C) 1/36
   (D) 1/44
   (E) 1/144
   (F) none of the above

7. A gene is to an allele as

   (A) Ice cream is to its various flavors
   (B) Genotypes are to phenotypes
   (C) Mutations are to DNA replication
   (D) Answer a & b
   (E) None of the above

8. If (B) is the dominant genotype for brown eyes and (b) is the recessive allele for blue eyes which of the following is true of the gametes produced by a person with the genotype Bb?

   (A) Half of them are B and half are b
   (B) Half of them are BB and half are Bb
   (C) All of them are BB
   (D) All of them are bb
   (E) None of the above

9. If (B) is the dominant genotype for brown eyes and (b) is the recessive allele for blue eyes which of the following is true of the gametes produced by a person with the genotype BB?

   (A) Half of them are B and half are b
   (B) Half of them are BB and half are Bb
   (C) All of them are B
   (D) All of them are BB
   (E) None of the above

10. If (B) is the dominant genotype for brown eyes and (b) is the recessive allele for blue eyes which of the following is true of the gametes produced by a person with the genotype Bb?

    (A) Half of them would be B
    (B) Half of them would be b
    (C) Half of them would have a brown eye allele
    (D) Half of them would have a blue eye allele
    (E) All of the above

Refer to the following choices for the next 4 consecutive questions.

(A) 0

(F) 1/16

(G) 3/16

(H) 9/16

(I) 1

In a particular species of flower the short gene (t) and the white petal gene (p) are on different chromosomes. The respective Tall gene (T) and the respective purple petal gene (P) exists on their respective loci on their respective chromosomes.

11. From a cross of PPTT and pptt what is the probability of having offspring with PpTt? __I__

12. From a cross of PPTT and pptt what is the probability of having offspring which show the short white phenotype?__A__

13. From a cross of PpTt and PpTt what is the probability of having offspring with the genotype pptt? __F__

14. From a cross of PpTt and PpTt what is the probability of having offspring that shows the tall purple phenotype? __H__

For the next 6 consecutive questions refer to the following statement:

In lilys the tall gene is dominant (A) over the recessive short allele (a) and the Red allele (Z) is incompletely dominant with the white allele (Z'). Heterozygous genotypes for petal color have a pink color.

15. If a homozygous dominant lily for height with red flowers is crossed with a short lilly with white flowers which choice best describes the genotypes and phenotypes that will be present in the F_1 generation

   (A) All AaZZ' (tall and pink)

   (B) All AaZZ (tall and red)

   (C) All AaZ'Z' (tall and white)

   (D) All aaZZ (short and red)

   (E) All aaZ'Z' (short and white)

16. What is the probability of lily's that have the genotype aaZZ' and AaZZ producing offspring that is a short white lily?

   (A) 0

   (B) ¼

   (C) ½

   (D) ¾

   (E) 1

17. What is the probability of lily's that have the genotype aaZZ' and AaZZ producing offspring that have the phenotypes of short and red?

   (A) 0

   (B) ¼

   (C) ½

   (D) ¾

   (E) 1

18. What is the probability of lily's that have the genotype aaZZ' and AaZZ producing offspring that have the phenotypes of tall and red?

   (A) 0

   (B) ¼

   (C) ½

   (D) ¾

   (E) 1

19. What is the probability of lily's that have the genotype aaZZ' and AaZZ producing offspring that have the phenotypes tall and pink

(A) 0
(B) ¼
(C) ½
(D) ¾
(E) 1

$$\frac{1}{2} \cdot \frac{1}{2}$$

20. What is the probability of lily's that have the genotype aaZZ' and AaZZ producing offspring that have the phenotypes short and pink

(A) 0
(B) ¼
(C) ½
(D) ¾
(E) 1

$$\frac{1}{7} \cdot \frac{1}{2}$$

21. What is the probability of the cross AaBbCCDd X AABBCCDd producing offspring that have the genotype AaBbCCdd?

(A) ¼
(B) 1/8
(C) 1/16
(D) ½
(E) 0

A A
A AA AA
a Aa Aa

$$\frac{1}{2} \cdot \frac{1}{2} \cdot 1 \cdot \frac{1}{4}$$

22. What is the probability of the cross AaBbCCDd X AABBCCDd producing offspring that have the genotype AABBCCDD?

(A) ¼
(B) 1/8
(C) 1/16
(D) ½
(E) 0

$$\frac{1}{2} \cdot \frac{1}{2} \cdot 1 \cdot \frac{1}{4}$$

Refer to the following choices when answering the next 6 consecutive questions. Answers can be used once, multiple times, or not at all.

(A) Pleiotropy

(F) Codominance

(G) Incomplete dominance

(H) Epistasis

(I) Mendelian inheritance

(J) Gene linkage

23. When two dominant and different alleles are crossed and the result is a blend of the two characteristics (i.e. red and white flowers producing pink flowers) this is said to be ____G____.

24. When two dominant and different alleles are crossed and the result is that both alleles are expressed separately. This type of dominance is said to be____F____.

25. When alleles at specific loci on a chromosome are located closer relative to other another loci these two genes tend to be inherited together because of the unlikeliness of a swap between the shorter distances. This phenomena best describes ____J____.

26. ____A____is when one gene affects the phenotypes of seemingly unrelated genes.

27. ____H____ is a genetic phenomenon in which one gene's expression modifies or suppresses the expression of another gene.

28. ____I____ uses Punnett squares to predict phenotypes and genotypes of a particular trait.

29. Let T and t represent two alleles for a specific gene and let S and s represent two alleles for a separate gene located on the same chromosome. Suppose an individual has one chromosome that has the T and S alleles and another chromosome that has the s and t alleles which of the following is true?

(A) Gametes from this individual could be homozygous dominant for both genes
(B) The two chromosomes must be homologous
(C) The genes must be linked
(D) Answer b &c
(E) All of the above

Refer to the following diagram of a chromosome with alleles for specific genes at specific loci to answer the following question.

Chromosome I: ·······a······················B·······C

Chromosome II: ·······A······················B·······c

30. Which of the following statements about the above diagram is false?

(A) Chromosome I and chromosome II must be homologous
(B) Chromosome II alleles A and B will be inherited in gametes more likely relative to alleles B and c.
(C) Allele C from chromosome I and allele c from chromosome II occur the same distance from the loci for gene A on both chromosomes.
(D) None of the above

For the next 2 consecutive questions base your answer on the below description of a fictional genetic defect:

The fictional genetic disorder lobster hands have the phenotype of having (on both hands) a person's index fingers attached to their middle fingers and their ring finger and their pinky finger are also connected.

31. From which parent(s) did a male with lobster hands inherit this trait if the trait is an x-linked recessive genetic disorder?

(A) Only the mother
(B) Other the father
(C) The father or the mother, but not both
(D) Both the father and the mother
(E) It is not possible to determine from the information given

32. Which of the following would be considered valid evidence for a conclusion that lobster hands is an autosomal recessive trait and not an X-linked trait?

(A) An affected mother and a homozygous dominant father produce unaffected offspring
(B) An affected father and a homozygous dominant mother produce unaffected offspring
(C) An affected mother and a homozygous dominant father produce unaffected male offspring
(D) An affected mother and a homozygous dominant father produce unaffected female
(E) It is not possible to determine from the information given

For the next 6 consecutive questions choose from the following choices

(A) Sickle celled anemia
(F) Hemophilia
(G) Down syndrome
(H) Turner syndrome
(I) Huntington's disease
(J) Red green color blindness

33. ___A___ is characterized by having an abnormality in the oxygen carrying molecule hemoglobin.

34. ___F___ and ___J___ are both recessive x-linked genetic diseases/disoders.

35. ___G___ is caused by an autosomal nondisjunction.

36. ___F___ has symptoms of affected individuals bleeding out due to an inability to clot effectively.

Huntington's

37. ___I___ is a neurological genetic disorder characterized by changes in behavior and usually onsets between age 35-44

38. ___A___ has an advantage for those who are heterozygous to the trait, they are immune to malaria

LEVEL 3 DIFFICULTY

39. The ability to be immune to virus XYZ is inherited through an autosomal dominant allele. What is the probability that a child descendent from parents both heterozygous for this trait can be immune to virus XYZ?

(A) 0
(B) ¼
(C) ½
(D) ¾
(E) 1

40. If rose flowers have the dominant allele for red petals (R) and the recessive allele for white petals (r) and two red rose flowers reproduced and made 40 flowers and 10 of them were white, what is the genotype for the parents?

(A) RR and RR
(B) RR and Rr
(C) Rr and Rr
(D) Rr and rr
(E) rr and rr

41. If pea plants have the dominant allele green (G) and the recessive allele yellow (g) and two green pea plants produced 100 pea plants with zero

yellow plants produced and 100% of them were green, the genotypes of the parents could have been

(A) RR and RR
(B) RR and Rr
(C) Rr and Rr
(D) Rr and rr
(E) rr and rr
(F) answer a &b
(G) none of the above

42. If (B) is the dominant genotype for brown eyes and (b) is the recessive allele for blue eyes which of the following is true of the gametes produced by a person with the genotype bb?

(A) Half of them are B and half are b
(B) Half of them are BB and half are Bb
(C) All of them are bb
(D) All of them are b
(E) None of the above

43. Suppose that a particular breed of dog has a dominant allele of (B) for black fur and (b) for white fur in the breeds gene pooland you happen to observe a black dog of this particular breed. Assuming the dog is a pure bread which of the following would be valid a conclusion?

(A) The dogs genotype for hair color
(B) The dogs phenotype for hair color
(C) The genotypes for one of its parents
(D) The phenotypes for both parents
(E) The genotypes for both parents

44. What is the probability of the cross AaBbCCDd X AABBCCDd producing offspring that has the genotype AaBBCcDD?

(A) ¼
(B) 1/8
(C) 1/16

$$A \quad A$$
$$A \quad AA \quad AA$$
$$a \quad Aa \quad Aa$$

(D) ½

(E) 0

45. People that are born with red hair often have fair skin. Which of the following can best explain this phenomenon?

(A) The two genes probably exist very close to one another on a chromosome

(B) The two genes are sex linked

(C) The two genes while very similar exhibit pleiotropic inheritance

(D) The two genes are codominant to one another

(E) The two genes are incompletely dominant to one another

MOLECULAR GENETICS

LEVEL 1 DIFFICULTY

1. The function of DNA replication is to
    (A) Ensure that the integrity of the genetic material stays in tact through out the next generation
    (B) Help to ensure that genetic information is passed down from one generation to the other
    (C) Copy DNA in S-phase of the cell cycle
    (D) All of the above

2. The ultimate conclusion of transcription is
    (A) A complimentary R-RNA molecule
    (B) A polypeptide
    (C) An amino acid
    (D) A complimentary M-RNA molecule
    (E) None of the above

3. The ultimate conclusion of translation is
    (A) A complimentary R-RNA molecule
    (B) A protein
    (C) A lipid based molecule
    (D) A complimentary M-RNA molecule
    (E) None of the above

4. Which of the following is the accepted form of DNA replication?
    (A) Semi conservative
    (B) Conservative
    (C) Dispersive
    (D) None of the above

5. In bacteria the circular DNA structure found outside the main DNA structure is called a
   (A) plasmid
   (B) chromosome
   (C) PCR
   (D) Nucleosome
   (E) Histone

6. Variation in a bacteria colony can manifest by
   (A) Crossing over events
   (B) Chiasmata
   (C) Mutation
   (D) Transformation
   (E) Answers c &d
   (F) All of the above

LEVEL 2 DIFFICULTY

7. The DNA molecule is double stranded. Each strand is able to be connected because of the presence of
   (A) Hydrogen bonds
   (B) Ionic bonds
   (C) Non-polar covalent bonds
   (D) Polar covalent bonds

8. Which of the following is true?
   (A) Guanine is a type of nucleic acid
   (B) Ribosomes contain guanine, uracil, adenine, cytosine and the building blocks to proteins
   (C) Some RNA molecules have a double helix structure
   (D) In plant cells DNA, RNA, and protein is synthesized in the nucleus
   (E) None of the above

9. Which of the following enzymes are involved in transcription and translation?

   (A) RNA polymerase

   (B) Helicase

   (C) DNA ligase

   (D) DNA polymerase

   (E) Primase

   (F) Answer a & b

   (G) All of the above

10. Which of the following molecules is in the same class of biological molecules and most similar to Adenine?

    (A) Helicase

    (B) Cellulose

    (C) ATP

    (D) Cholesterol

    (E) None of the above

11. When a series of samples of DNA undergo gel electrophoresis

    (A) Larger sections of DNA move faster than smaller sections of DNA

    (B) Smaller sections of DNA move faster than larger sections of DNA but the smaller sections don't move as far

    (C) Smaller sections of DNA move faster than large sections of DNA and they travel longer distances relative to larger sections

    (D) Enzymes are used to stain the DNA fragments so that they can be seen better

    (E) none of the above

12. In the process of protein synthesis a DNA molecule is to a blue print as a ribosome is to

    (A) A construction worker

    (B) A house

    (C) A brick

    (D) None of the above

13. In the process of protein synthesis a DNA molecule is to a blue print as a protein is to

    (A) A construction worker
    (B) A house
    (C) A brick
    (D) None of the above

14. In the process of protein synthesis a DNA molecule is to a blue print as an amino acid is to

    (A) A construction worker
    (B) A house
    (C) A brick
    (D) None of the above

Base you answers to the next 5 consecutive questions on the diagram provided below:

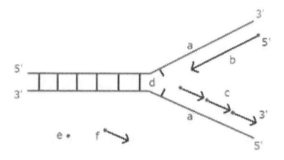

For the intents and purposes of these questions we will call "a" on top "a₁" and the "a" on the bottom "a₂".

15. The above diagram is an illustration of

(A) Protein synthesis

(B) Transcription

(C) Translation

(D) DNA replication

(E) All of the above

16. Structure b is the

(A) Leading strand

(B) Lagging strand

(C) Point where helicase acts on DNA

(D) Site of okazaki fragments

(E) None of the above

17. Structure c is best described as the

(A) Leading strand

(B) Lagging strand

(C) Point where helicase acts on DNA

(D) Site where RNA primase acts on DNA

(E) None of the above

18. DNA is always copied

(A) From 5' to 3'

(B) From 3' to 5'

(C) Toward the direction of the helicase enzyme

(D) Where ever T-RNA dictates

(E) None of the above

19. Which letter best describes where DNA has helicase act on it?

(A) a₁

(B) a₂

(C) b

(D) c

(E) d

20. Which of the following codes for an amino acid?

(A) DNA ligase

(B) RNA polymerase

(C) M-RNA

(D) T-RNA

(E) None of the above

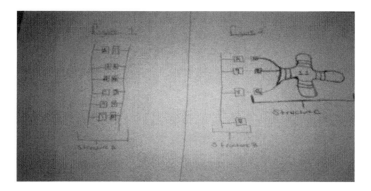

For the next 9 consecutive questions refer to the above diagram.

21. From the information provided structure labeled 7 is most likely

    (A) Adenine

    (B) Guanine

    (C) Cytosine

    (D) A nucleotide

    (E) Thymine or uracil

22. Structure A is most likely

    (A) A DNA molecule

    (B) An RNA molecule

    (C) A protein

    (D) An enzyme

23. Structure B is made

    (A) In the cytoplasm of the cell

    (B) In the nucleus

    (C) In the mitochondria

    (D) Answer a &b

    (E) All of the above

24. Both structure C and structure 11 depict

    (A) T-RNA

    (B) M-RNA

    (C) DNA

    (D) DNA ligase

    (E) None of the above

25. In structure A the box labeled 1 is most likely

   (A) Adenine

   (B) Guanine

   (C) Cytosine

   (D) Thymine

   (E) Uracil

26. In structure A the box labeled 3 is most likely

   (A) Adenine

   (B) Guanine

   (C) Cytosine

   (D) Thymine

   (E) Uracil

27. Which of the following does figure 2 depict

   (A) A step in the cell cycle

   (B) A step in S-phase

   (C) DNA replication

   (D) A step in protein synthesis

   (E) None of the above

28. In figure 2 the box labeled 10 is most likely

   (A) Adenine

   (B) Guanine

   (C) Cytosine

   (D) Thymine

   (E) Uracil

29. In figure 2 the box labeled 8 is most likely

  (A) Adenine

  (B) Guanine

  (C) Cytosine

  (D) Thymine

  (E) Uracil

30. The instructions that are used to eventually build a protein but first build an amino acid is brought to the ribosome by the

  (A) DNA

  (B) M-RNA

  (C) R-RNA

  (D) All of the above

  (E) None of the above

31. Which of the following describes the conservative hypothesis for DNA replication?

  (A) Each old strand acts as a template to form a new strand

  (B) Each strand in the daughter DNA would consist of a mixture of old and new DNA

  (C) The original molecule could remain in tact after synthesis, so that the product molecule would consist of two newly formed DNA strands

  (D) None of the above describe the conservative hypothesis for DNA replication

32. Base your answer on the following: A virus was found to have the following nucleic acid percentages:

Nucleic acid	Percent
Adenine	22.8%
Thymine	32.8%
Guanine	40.1%
Cytosine	4.3

The molecule is most likely

(A) Double stranded DNA

(B) Mitochondrial DNA

(C) Messenger RNA

(D) T- RNA

(E) Single stranded DNA

33. Which of the following are valid conclusions for the work that Griffith did on streptococcus pneumonia in mice?

(A) R-strain killed the mice

(B) S-strain is virulent

(C) Live R-strain were transformed into S-strain

(D) Answer a & c

(E) Answer b & c

34. Which of the following best describes what is found at the other end of a free phosphate found at the 5' end of a DNA strand?

(A) A hydroxyl group on the 5' carbon of a deoxyribose sugar.

(B) A hydroxyl group on the 3' carbon of a deoxyribose sugar.

(C) A phosphate group on the 5' carbon of a deoxyribose sugar.

(D) A phosphate group on the 3' carbon of a deoxyribose sugar.

(E) A base attached to the 3' carbon of a deoxyribose sugar.

35. Which of the following best describes the reason for DNA moving through out the agarose gel in gel electrophoresis?

  (A) DNA is a positive molecule and it is attracted to the negative end of the aparatus due to an electric current
  (B) DNA is a negative molecule and it is attracted to the negative end of the apparatus due to a magnetic field
  (C) DNA is a negative molecule and it is attracted to the positive end of the apparatus due to an electric current
  (D) DNA is a positive molecule and it is attracted to the negative end of the aparatus due to a magnetic field
  (E) None of the above

36. Which of the following is true of T-RNA molecules
  (A) They possess a 3' acceptor stem used in binding to amino acids
  (B) They are the main component of ribosomes
  (C) Anti-codons of T-RNA molecules have the ability to base-pair to more than one type of codon
  (D) Answer a & c
  (E) All of the above

37. Which of the following will have the greatest effect on gene expression?
  (A) A frame shift
  (B) A deletion
  (C) A substitution
  (D) Cannot be determined from the following information

38. Which of the following will most likely cause the greatest affect on cell function
  (A) A single nucleotide is substituted throughout a DNA strand
  (B) A single nucleotide is added throughout a DNA strand
  (C) Insertion of a triplet of nucleotides in a DNA strand
  (D) A deletion of a triplet of nucleotides in a DNA strand
  (E) Cannot be determined from the information provided

EVOLUTION

1. Which of the following describes the details of how populations of organisms change from generation to generation and how new species originate?
   (A) Microevolution
   (B) Macroevolution
   (C) Sympatric speciation
   (D) Allopatric speciation
   (E) None of the above

2. Which of the following describes patterns of change in groups of related species over broad periods of geologic time. The patterns determine phylogeny, the evolutionary relationships among species and groups of species?
   (A) Microevolution
   (B) Macroevolution
   (C) Sympatric speciation
   (D) Allopatric speciation
   (E) None of the above

3. Which of the following evolutionary scientists employed the theory of use and disuse?
   (A) Lamareck
   (B) Darwin
   (C) Malthus
   (D) Wallace

4. All of the following are postulates to Lamarek's theory of evolution except

   (A) Use and disuse
   (B) Inheritance of acquired characteristics
   (C) Natural transformation of species
   (D) Traits must be heritable
   (E) None of the above

5. All of the following are postulates to Darwin's theory of evolution except

   (A) Traits must be heritable
   (B) Individuals must vary within a population
   (C) Natural transformation of species
   (D) Over production of offspring
   (E) Some characteristics must better enable individuals to survive
   (F) None of the above

6. Which of the following occurred as a direct result of photosynthesizing organisms arising?

   (A) The end to chemical evolution
   (B) The end of the Cambrian explosion
   (C) The start of the Cambrian explosion
   (D) The rise of multicellular sexually reproducing organisms
   (E) None of the above

7. Adaptations are acquired through out populations by

   (A) Mutations
   (B) Genetic drift
   (C) Hardy Weinberg principle
   (D) Natural selection
   (E) Sexual reproduction

8. A mutation can be passed down from one generation to another in sexually reproducing organisms by the mutation occurring in

   (A) A somatic cell

(B) A gamete

(C) An autosome

(D) A skin cell

(E) None of the above

9. When a gene travels from one continent to another it is considered to be

(A) Gene flow

(B) Genetic drift

(C) Survival of the fittest

(D) Sexual selection

(E) none of the above

10. A bird having bright coloration will likely perpetuate

(A) Sexual selection

(B) Artificial selection

(C) Gene flow

(D) Genetic drift

(E) None of the above

11. A population of flowers consists of 98 white flowers out of a total population of 200. White is recessive and red is dominant. What percent of the population would be heterozygotes?

(A) 45%

(B) 58%

(C) 42%

(D) 49%

(E) 9%

12. A population of flowers consists of 98 white flowers out of a total population of 200. White is recessive and red is dominant. What percent of the population would be either homozygous dominant or homozygous recessive?

(A) 45%

(B) 58%

(C) 42%

13. A population of flowers consists of 98 white flowers out of a total population of 200. White is recessive and red is dominant. What percent of the population would be homozygous dominant?

(A) 45%

(B) 58%

(C) 42%

(D) 49%

(E) 9%

(F) none of the above

14. A population wild Dingo has the spotted coat allele, which is dominant, and the non-spotted allele, which is recessive. If the frequencies of homozygous dominant, heterozygous, and homozygous recessive individuals for this trait were 32%, 65%, and 3% respectively. The frequencies of the dominant and the recessive alleles frequencies must be

(A) $\sqrt{32}$ and $1-\sqrt{32}$ respectively

(B) .32 and .68 respectively

(C) .32 and .65 respectively

(D) $\sqrt{65}$ and $\sqrt{3}$ respectively

(E) Cannot be determined from the information provided

15. A particular type of butterfly has a series of characteristics on their wings. They are pointed edges and rounded edges, black with brown spots, and black with red spots. The various patterns and frequencies of all of the above characteristics could be attributed by all of the following except:

(A) Natural selection

(B) Convergent evolution

(C) A balanced polymorphism

(D) Mutations

(E) Random chance

16. All of the following are homologous structures except:

(A) Dolphin flipper

(B) Human arm

(C) Bears front foot

(D) Birds wing

(E) Butterfly wing

17. Which of the following pairs are considered analogous structures to one another?

(A) A butterfly wing and an eagles wing

(B) A human arm and a whales arm

(C) Dolphin flipper and a horses front leg

(D) Alligator leg and a deer's leg

(E) None of the above

18. All of the following are considered sources of evidence for evolution except

(A) Homologous structrues

(B) The fossil record

(C) Embryology

(D) Analogous structures

(E) Inheritance of acquired characteristics

19. Comparative Molecular Biology

(A) Is a source of evidence for evolution

(B) Compares lipids between different but closely related species

(C) Compares nucleotide and amino acid sequences between different but closely related species

(D) Answer a & b

(E) Answer a & c

(F) All of the above

Use the following choices to answer the next 6 consecutive questions. Answers can be used once, multiple times, or not at all.

(A) Allopatric speciation

(G) Sympatric speciation

(H) Adaptive radiation

(I) Sexual reproduction

(J) Directional selection

(K) Bottleneck

Base your answers for the next 6 consecutive questions on the above choices

20. A foot fungus becomes resistant to an athletes foot spray on medication. This fungus then increases in population. _____

21. A species of salamanders diverge over a period of tens of thousands of years as a result of a mountain range emerging during this time. _____

22. When temperatures decrease in a particular habitat many new forms and variations arise as a result due to the new selective pressures present. _____

23. About 70,000 years ago there was a super volcanic explosion, which caused the population of humans to be reduced to 15,000 individuals. _____

24. The ultimate source of variation. _____

25. Three different variations of beak sizes among the same population of finches within the same island. _____

26. Stanley Miller tested the theories associated with

(A) Evolution via natural selection

(B) Evolution via punctuated equilibrium

(C) Primordial soup and the origin of life

(D) Adaptive radiation

(E) None of the above

Base your answer to the next two consecutive questions on the following diagram:

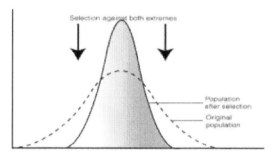

27. The above graph shows selection patterns favoring the

(A) lower extreme

(B) higher extreme

(C) median

(D) cannot be determined because the characteristic is not specified

28. The above graph is an example of a trait exhibiting

(A) Stabilizing selection

(B) Disruptive selection

(C) Directional selection

(D) None of the above

Base your answer to the next 2 consecutive questions on the following diagram:

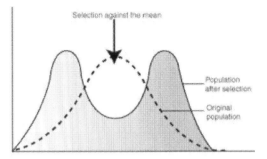

29. The above graph shows selection patterns favoring the

(A) lower extreme

(B) higher extreme

(C) median

(D) answer a & b

(E) all of the above

30. The above graph is an example of a trait exhibiting

(A) Stabilizing selection

(B) Disruptive selection

(C) Directional selection

(D) None of the above

31. Genetic drift occurs

(A) Randomly by allele frequencies changing within a population over time

(B) When migration occurs and different selective pressures occur on the migrated portion of the population

(C) By allele frequencies changing in a population due to sexual selection patterns

(D) By disruptive selection patterns

(E) None of the above

32. Pentadactyl limbs are examples of

(A) Homologous structures

(B) Analogous structures

(C) Convergent evolution

(D) Divergent evolution

(E) None of the above

33. Mutations appearance in a population is

(A) Due to natural selection

(B) Due to random chance

(C) Due to directional selection

(D) An event that while rare can be beneficial

(E) Answer b & d

(F) Answer a & d

34. Earth's primordial atmosphere consisted of all of the following except

(A) CO

(B) CO_2

(C) HCl (hydrochloric acid)

(D) Sulfur

(E) O_2

Base the following 4 consecutive questions on the below choices. For each question choose the answer that is best described. Each answer can be used once, multiple times, or not at all.

(A) Divergent evolution

(F) Convergent evolution

(G) Parallel evolution

(H) Coevolution

35. A type of evolution often seen in a predator prey relationship where a prey species may evolve a trait that enables them to escape 99% of the predator population but the 1% of the predator population will then select for the trait that enables for them to catch their prey. _____

36. Two related lineages or two related populations that have made similar evolutionary changes after a divergence. _____

37. Describes two unrelated species that have similar traits as a result of independently adapting to similar ecological conditions. Often analogous traits are seen between these two species. _____

38. Two unrelated species that become increasingly different over time. _____

BIOLOGICAL DIVERSITY

1. Which of the following taxa contains organisms that are most closely related?

   (A) Order
   (B) Class
   (C) Family
   (D) Kingdom
   (E) Phylum

2. Finish the following sentence so that it is correct: Prokaryotic DNA is not associated with_____.

   (A) Adenine
   (B) Thymine
   (C) Histone proteins
   (D) The same nucleotides as eukaryotes
   (E) None of the above

For the next 7 consecutive questions base your answers off the below choices:

   (A) nitrogen fixing enzymes
   (F) Parasitic bacteria
   (G) spirochetes
   (H) Nitrifying bacteria
   (I) Nitrogen-fixing bacteria
   (J) Cyanobacteria
   (K) Carbon fixing enzymes

3. Some chemosynthetic bacteria are also called

4. This type of bacteria is photosynthetic and they have specialized cells called heterocysts

5. Feed off of their host usually without killing it usually

6. Contain accessory pigments called phycoblins

7. Have flagella within the layers of the cell wall

8. Cyanobacteria produce

9. Have a mutualistic relationship with plants

10. All of the following are not found in bacteria except
   (A) Phycobilins
   (B) Chloroplast
   (C) Nucleus
   (D) Nucleosomes
   (E) None of the above

11. Which of the following are considered to be photosynthetic?
   (A) Foraminifera
   (B) Cyanobacteria
   (C) Nitrogen fixing bacteria
   (D) Rhizopoda
   (E) None of the above

12. Apicomplexans lack

    (A) Apical complex structure
    (B) Motility
    (C) Spores
    (D) Organelles
    (E) None of the above

13. All of the following are part of the kingdom Fungi except

    (A) Ascomycota
    (B) Lichens
    (C) Deutoromycota
    (D) glomeromycota
    (E) None of the above

14. In _____ early cleavage occur straight down in a radial form

    (A) Protostomes
    (B) Deuterostomes
    (C) Chordates
    (D) Answer a & b
    (E) None of the above

15. All of the following are types of Platyhelminthes except

    (A) Flatworms
    (B) Round worms
    (C) Flukes
    (D) Tapeworms
    (E) None of the above

16. Which of the following has two germ layers?

    (A) Cnidaria

    (B) Mollusca

    (C) Porifera

    (D) Chordate

    (E) Rotifer

    (F) None of the above

17. Which of the following is an example of mutualism?

    (A) Pasmodial slime molds

    (B) Flatworms living in an animals gut

    (C) Nitrogen –fixing bacteria in nodules

    (D) A cow birds relationship to other birds

18. Conidia is a structure in fungi that

    (A) Produces male gametes

    (B) Produces female gametes

    (C) Carries out asexual reproduction

    (D) Consumes nutrients/ food

    (E) None of the above

19. Flowering plants are associated with all of the following except

    (A) Gymnosperms

    (B) Stamens

    (C) Petals

    (D) Sepals

    (E) Anther

20. Which of the following is the male reproductive structure in flowing plants?

    (A) Pistil
    (B) Stamen
    (C) Style
    (D) Stigma
    (E) None of the above

21. All of the following are characteristics of the kingdom animalia except

    (A) Multicellular
    (B) Heterotrophic
    (C) Motility
    (D) The dominant generation in the life cycle of animals is the haploid generation
    (E) Most animals undergo a period of embryonic development during which two or three layers of tissues form

22. Which of the following nourishes an embryo in angiosperms ?

    (A) synergids
    (B) The fruit
    (C) Antheridium
    (D) Endosperm
    (E) None of the above

23. A fruit is produced by

    (A) Angiosperms
    (B) Gymnosperms
    (C) Bryophytes
    (D) Lycophyta
    (E) All of the above

24. Pharyngeal gill slits are common in all
   (A) Animals
   (B) Chordates
   (C) Annelida
   (D) Arthropoda
   (E) Answer a &b

25. Which of the following has a notochord?
   (A) Chordates
   (B) Annelida
   (C) Mollusca
   (D) Nematode
   (E) None of the above

26. All of the following are coelomates except
   (A) Annelida
   (B) Chordate
   (C) Mollusca
   (D) Rotifer
   (E) Echinodermata

27. They phyla Annelida includes all of the following except
   (A) Leeches
   (B) Earthworms
   (C) Polychaete worms
   (D) Flukes
   (E) None of the above

28. Which of the following can have both medusa and polyp stages within their life cycle?

  (A) Chordates
  (B) Platyhelminthes
  (C) Cnidaria
  (D) Rotifera
  (E) Echinodermata

29. Which of the following has radial symmetry?

  (A) Cnidarians
  (B) Mollusca
  (C) Chordate
  (D) rotifera
  (E) None of the above

30. Which of the following are acoelomates?

  (A) Platyhelminthes
  (B) Nematode
  (C) Chordates
  (D) Annelida
  (E) None of the above

31. Which of the following are deuterostomes?

  (A) Echinoderms
  (B) Chordates
  (C) Arthropoda
  (D) Annelida
  (E) Answer a & b
  (F) All of the above

PLANTS

LEVEL 2 DIFFICULTY

1. Xylem is a structure in plants that

    (A) Transports water
    (B) Is dead at functional maturity
    (C) Transports sugar
    (D) Answer a & b
    (E) Answer b & c

2. Dicots differ from monocots in that

    (A) Dicots have two cotyledons
    (B) Dicots have a taproot
    (C) Dicots have 4- 5 petals or multiples thereof
    (D) Dicots have netted leaf venation
    (E) All of the above

3. Monocots have

    (A) Parallel venation
    (B) Scattered vascular bundles
    (C) 3 cotyledons
    (D) a tap root
    (E) answer a & b

4. Transpiration is a process that is necessary for plants to survive but it occurs at a cost to the plant. Which of the following describes both why it is necessary and why there is a "cost" to the plant as well?

   (A) Transpiration is a process that allows the plant to take in CO_2. This occurs by means of the guard cells opening stomata and photons are lost to the environment

   (B) Transpiration is a process that allows the plant to take in O_2. This occurs by means of the guard cells opening stomata and photons are lost to the environment

   (C) Transpiration is a process that allows the plant to take in CO_2. This occurs by means of the guard cells opening stomata and water is lost to the environment

   (D) Transpiration is a process that allows the plant to take in O_2. This occurs by means of the guard cells opening stomata and water is lost to the environment

   (E) None of the above

5. Vascular bundles occurring in a circle like pattern is a characteristic of

   (A) Monocots
   (B) Dicots
   (C) Plants that also have 3 petals or multiples thereof
   (D) Answer a & c
   (E) Answer b & c

6. The cortex

   (A) Lines the outside surface of the root
   (B) Makes up the bulk of the root
   (C) Is a band of fatty material
   (D) Is used for sugar transport

7. A corn plant will have

   (A) A taproot, leaves with netted venation, and two cotyledons
   (B) A taproot, leaves with netted venation, and one cotyledon
   (C) A fibrous root system, leaves with parallel venation, and one cotyledon
   (D) A fibrous root system, netted venation, and one cotyledon

(E) None of the above

8. Phloem is
   (A) Used to transport soluble organic material
   (B) Used to transport water
   (C) Dead at maturity
   (D) All of the above
   (E) None of the above

9. Which of the following functions as a means of connecting the cytoplasm from one plant cell to another?
   (A) Plasmodesmata
   (B) Suberin
   (C) Epidermis
   (D) Spongy mesophyll
   (E) Guard cells

10. All of the following help plants grow except
    (A) gibberellins
    (B) Auxin
    (C) Hydrogen ion
    (D) Abscisic acid

11. Choose the answer that best finishes the sentence: Auxin is produced in the _____ and moves downward by _____ into the zone of elongation and generates growth by stimulating elongation.
    (A) Apical meristem, passive transport
    (B) Apical meristem, active transport
    (C) Lateral meristem, passive transport
    (D) Lateral meristem, active transport

12. Primary growth occurs in

   (A) Lateral meristems
   (B) Apical meristems
   (C) Cork cambium
   (D) Vascular cambium
   (E) Answers a, c, &d are all correct

13. Secondary growth occurs in

   (A) Lateral meristems
   (B) Apical meristems
   (C) Cork cambium
   (D) Vascular cambium
   (E) Answers a, c, &d are all correct

14. Stripping a 360 degree ring of bark around a tree will ultimately cause the tree to die because

   (A) The xylem cells, which carry water through the plant, were stripped from the tree
   (B) The xylem cells, which carry sugar through the plant, were stripped from the tree
   (C) The phloem cells, which carry soluble organic material, were stripped from the tree
   (D) The phloem cells, which carry water, were stripped from the tree
   (E) None of the above

For the next consecutive questions base your answers on the image below of a generalized flower

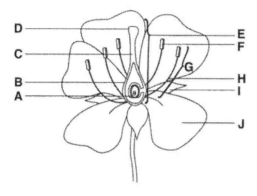

15. Letter A represents the

   (A) Ovary
   (B) Ovule
   (C) Stamen
   (D) Pistil
   (E) Style

16. Letter B represents the

   (A) Ovary
   (B) Ovule
   (C) Style
   (D) Stamen
   (E) Stigma

17. Letter C represents the

    (A) Ovary

    (B) Ovule

    (C) Style

    (D) Stamen

    (E) Stigma

18. Letter D represents the

    (A) Ovary

    (B) Ovule

    (C) Style

    (D) Stamen

    (E) Stigma

19. Letter E represents the

    (A) Stamen

    (B) Pistil

    (C) Anther

    (D) Filament

    (E) Sepal

20. Structure F represents the

    (A) Stamen

    (B) Pistil

    (C) Anther

    (D) Filament

    (E) Sepal

21. Structure G represents the

    (A) Stamen

    (B) Pistil

    (C) Anther

    (D) Filament

    (E) Sepal

22. Structure H represents the

    (A) Stamen

    (B) Pistil

    (C) Anther

    (D) Filament

    (E) Sepal

23. Structure I represents the

    (A) Petals

    (B) Sepals

    (C) Anther

    (D) Stem

    (E) stigma

24. Structure J represents the

    (A) Petals

    (B) Sepals

    (C) Stamen

    (D) Pistil

    (E) Anther

25. The function of J is

   (A) To provide male gametes to the ovary
   (B) To attract pollinators
   (C) To receive male gametes for fertilization
   (D) None of the above

26. The primary function of structure F is

   (A) To bear the pollen
   (B) To hold the male gametes
   (C) To attract pollinators
   (D) Answers a & b
   (E) All of the above

27. The pistil consists of the

   (A) stigma and style which are the male reproductive structures
   (B) Stigma and style which are the female reproductive structures
   (C) Anther and the filament which are male reproductive organs
   (D) Anther and the filament which are female reproductive organs
   (E) None of the above

28. The stamen consists of the

   (A) stigma and style which are the male reproductive structures
   (B) Stigma and style which are the female reproductive structures
   (C) Anther and the filament which are male reproductive organs
   (D) Anther and the filament which are female reproductive organs
   (E) None of the above

29. Xylem cells consist of

(A) Two types of cells, vessel elements, and tracheids

(B) Two types of cells, sclereids, and tracheids

(C) Vessel members only

(D) Tracheids only

(E) None of the above

30. Phloem cells are called

(A) sieve tube members

(B) plasmodesmata

(C) tracheids

(D) vessel elements

(E) none of the above

31. During water transport through xylem what property regarding water makes it possible for water to be transported in a polymer like state?

(A) Water is a polar molecule

(B) Water molecules form hydrogen bonds

(C) Water has uneven distribution of electrons within the molecule

(D) Water molecules are attracted to other water molecules

(E) All of the above

ANIMAL FORM AND FUNCTION

1. Which of the following is most closely associated with transplanted tissue being damaged or destroyed by the immune system
   (A) MHC
   (B) Histamine
   (C) Interferons
   (D) Antibiotics

2. Drinking alcohol results in
   (A) Vasoconstriction which increases body temperature
   (B) Vasoconstriction which decreases body temperature
   (C) Vasodilatation which decreases body temperature
   (D) Vasodilation which increases body temperature
   (E) None of the above

3. Countercurrents are used in nature. Which of the following is not an example of a countercurrent?
   (A) Gas exchange in humans
   (B) Gas exchange in fish
   (C) The loop of Henle in the nephron
   (D) Blood movement in the legs of wading birds
   (E) Movement of blood in marine mamals

4. In humans HCO$_3$ is the _____ carrying molecule in the blood

   (A) Glycoprotein

   (B) Hemoglobin

   (C) Carbon dioxide

   (D) Answers a & b

   (E) All of the above

5. The respiratory and circulatory system is closely related. They ultimately join at

   (A) The diaphragm

   (B) Avleoli

   (C) The larynx

   (D) Spiracles

   (E) Bronchi

6. O$_2$ and CO$_2$ are exchanged between the respiratory system and the circulatory system by the process of

   (A) Diffusion

   (B) Active transport

   (C) Osmosis

   (D) Facilitated diffusion

   (E) None of the above

7. In response to a stimulus, gated ion channels in the membrane suddenly open and permit Na$^+$ on the outside to rush into the cell. As the positively charged Na$^+$ rush in, the charge on the cell membrane becomes depolarized, or more positive on the inside. This best describes

   (A) hyperpolarization

   (B) action potential

   (C) repolarization

   (D) refractory period

   (E) none of the above

For the next 6 consecutive questions use the following choices for answers. Choices can be used once, multiple times, or not at all.

(A) Nephron
(F) Kidney
(G) Urethra
(H) Urine
(I) Ureter
(J) Bladder

8. This is the structure that holds urine. _____

9. This is basic structural and functional unit of the kidney. _____

10. This structure consists of millions of individual filtering tubes _____.

11. This is the structure that acts as a bridge for urine from the kidneys to the bladder. _____

12. Urine is ultimately excreted in humans through the _____.

13. This is the waste fluid in humans. _____

Refer to the following choices to answer the next 6 consecutive questions

(A) Glomerulus
(B) Collecting duct
(C) Ascending limb
(D) Bowman's capsule
(E) Renal pelvis

14. The nephron tube begins with a bulb-shaped body at one end called the _____.

15. When the filtrate moves up in the _____ it becomes more dilute due to active and passive transport of salts out of the tubule.

16. Urine ultimately leaves the kidneys in this structure and then empty into the ureters. _____

17. A branch of the renal artery enters into the Bowman's capsule to form essentially a dense ball of capillaries this dense ball of capillaries is called the _____.

18. The _____ is connected to the distal convoluted tubule which eventually forms into the loop of Henle.

19. The left ventricle is responsible for
    (A) Maintaining Systolic blood pressure
    (B) Maintaining Diastolic blood pressure
    (C) Preventing blood from moving back into the ventricle
    (D) None of the above

20. When the filtrate moves down the descending limb it becomes
    (A) More concentrated due to active transport of water out of it
    (B) Less concentrated due to passive transport of water out of it
    (C) More concentrated due to passive transport of water out of it
    (D) More dilute due to active transport of water out of it
    (E) None of the above

21. In humans double capillary beds are found in all of the following except
    (A) The hypothalamus
    (B) The anterior pituitary gland
    (C) The glomerulus
    (D) The lungs
    (E) The liver

22. Which of the following choices is not involved in digestion?

   (A) The teeth
   (B) The pancreas
   (C) The stomach
   (D) The intestines
   (E) The duodenum

23. Pepsin is a(n)

   (A) Enzyme found in the kidneys
   (B) Enzyme found in the digestive tract
   (C) A glycoprotein found on the surface of cells in order to help the immune system differentiate self from invader
   (D) A structural protein in animal cells
   (E) None of the above

24. An action potential or nerve impulse has both electrical and chemical properties. Which of the following is essentially the chemical message produced that travels between neurons and muscle tissue?

   (A) A hormone
   (B) Calcium ion
   (C) Hydrogen ion
   (D) Acetylcholine
   (E) None of the above

25. Which of the following occurs during hyperpolarization?

   (A) An excess of K^+ Ions move out of the cell
   (B) In response to the inflow of Na^+, another kind of gated channel opens, this time allowing the K^+ on the inside to rush out of the cell
   (C) Calcium ions enter the cell
   (D) Neurotransmitters diffuse across the synaptic cleft and bindswith proteins on the postsynaptic membrane
   (E) None of the above

26. If the postsynaptic neuron is inhibited

(A) Only K+ ion gates open on the postsynaptic membrane

(B) Only Na+ ion gates open on the postsynaptic membrane

(C) An excitatory postsynaptic potential is established

(D) Ca+2 is released

(E) None of the above

27. Which of the following is not directly involved in regulating blood sugar levels?

(A) The pancreas

(B) Glucagon

(C) Angiotensin

(D) Insulin

28. Corpes becoming stiff is most directly due to

(A) Sugar no longer being broken down into pyruvate

(B) ATP is no longer being generated

(C) ADP and Pi are released and sliding motion of actin results

(D) Answers b & c

(E) None of the above

29. Which of the following is not part of the sliding filament model?

(A) ATP binds to a myosin head and forms ADP + Pi

(B) Ca+2 exposes the binding sites on the actin filaments

(C) Cross bridges between myosin heads and actin filaments form

(D) ATP causes the cross bridge to bind

(E) None of the above

30. Which of the following does not get digested in humans

(A) cellulose

(B) protein

(C) starches

(D) fats

(E) nucleic acids

31. All of the following hormones are involved in the digestive process except

(A) Cholecystokinin

(B) Secretin

(C) gastrin

(D) Angiotensinogen

REPRODUCTION AND DEVELOPMENT

LEVEL 2 DIFFICULTY

1. In humans gametogenesis occurs in the

   (A) Ovaries
   (B) Testes
   (C) Uterus
   (D) Bladder
   (E) Answer a &b

2. Spermatogenesis occurs in the

   (A) Ovaries
   (B) Uterus
   (C) Fallopian tube
   (D) Testes
   (E) None of the above

3. The epididymis is the site of

   (A) Semen production
   (B) Sperm production
   (C) Egg production
   (D) Sperm maturation
   (E) None of the above

4. Sperm is stored in the

   (A) Testes
   (B) Prostate
   (C) Epididymis
   (D) Ovaries
   (E) Vas deferens

5. Oogenesis or egg production starts

    (A) At birth
    (B) During puberty
    (C) During embryonic development
    (D) Through out the menstrual cycle
    (E) Upon zygote formation

For the next 6 consecutive questions refer to the choices below. Answers can be used once, multiple times, or not at all.

    (A) Luteinizing hormone (LH)
    (F) Testosterone
    (G) Progesterone
    (H) Follicle stimulating hormone (FSH)
    (I) Gonadotropin releasing hormone (GnRH)

6. The hormone that bridges the hypothalamus and the anterior pituitary gland in females. _____

7. The hormone that stimulates the development of the follicle is _____

8. Stimulates egg production. _____

9. The corpus luteum releases this hormone. _____

10. Signals the testes to produce androgens _____

11. This hormone develops the endometrium. _____

12. The storage of enzymes used for penetrating the egg during fertilization occurs in

   (A)   The acrosome within a sperm cells tail
   (B)   The acrosome within the sperms head
   (C)   The nucleus within the sperms head
   (D)   The Mitochondrion
   (E)   None of the above

13. Which of the following does an oocyte need to recognize before a sperm cell can enter?

   (A)   Protein
   (B)   Blastula
   (C)   Carbohydrate
   (D)   Glycoprotein
   (E)   None of the above

14. In human females how many viable cells usually develop from a single somatic cell that undergoes meiosis?

   (A)   1
   (B)   2
   (C)   3
   (D)   4
   (E)   none of the above

15. The center cavity formed by gastrulation is called

   (A)   The archenteron
   (B)   Ectoderm
   (C)   Endoderm
   (D)   Mesoderm
   (E)   None of the above

16. The type of blastula that is called a blastodisc is associated with

    (A) birds
    (B) reptiles
    (C) frogs
    (D) answers a & b
    (E) all of the above

17. Amniotes have extraembryonic membranes. Which of the following is not an extraembryonic membrane found in amniotes?

    (A) Yolk sac
    (B) Chorion
    (C) amnion
    (D) Allantois
    (E) None of the above

18. Which of the following best describes meiotic division in human females?

    (A) A process that produces 4 genetically different oocytes from one somatic cell
    (B) A process that produces 1 genetically different oocyte from one somatic cell
    (C) A process that produces 1 genetically different oocyte and 3 polar bodies from 1 somatic cell
    (D) A process that produces 1 genetically identical oocyte and 3 polar bodies from 1 somatic cell
    (E) None of the above

19. When animals that are not the same species attempt to mate what stops a sperm cell from fusing with the egg most likely?

    (A) The egg does not recognize protein secretions from the sperm cell
    (B) The egg does not recognize glycoprotein secretions from the sperm cell
    (C) The sperm cell does not recognize protein secretions from the egg cell
    (D) The sperm cell does not recognize glycoprotein secretions from the egg cell
    (E) None of the above

For the following 6 questions base your answer on the diagram of the female reproductive system below. Answers can be used once, multiple times, or not at all.

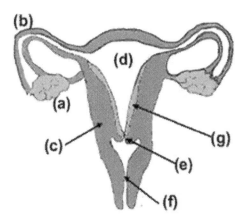

20. Which of the above letters represent the structure where fertilization usually occurs?

(A) A

(B) B

(C) C

(D) D

(E) E

(F) F

(G) G

(H) None of the above

21. Which of the above letters represent the endometrium?

(A) A

(B) B

(C) C

(D) D

(E) E

(F) F

(G) G

(H) None of the above

22. Which of the above letters represents the structure that receives the male sex organ during coitus?

(A) A

(B) B

(C) C

(D) D

(E) E

(F) F

(G) G

(H) None of the above

23. Which of the above letters represents the structure that allows a female to expel urine?

(A) A

(B) B

(C) C

(D) D

(E) E

(F) F

(G) G

(H) None of the above

24. Which of the above letters represents the site of oogenesis?

(A) A

(B) B

(C) C

(D) D

(E) E

(F) F

(G) G

(H) None of the above

25. Which of the above letters represents the tissue that the placenta forms from?

(A) A

(B) B

(C) C

(D) D

(E) E

(F) F

(G) G

(H) None of the above

26. In chordates cells along the dorsal surface of the mesoderm germ layer form the

(A) notochord

(B) trophoblast

(C) coelom

(D) answer a & b

(E) none of the above

Base your answers to the next 6 consecutive questions on the following diagram of the male reproductive system. Numbers can be used once, multiple times or not at all.

Male Reproductive System and Organs

27. Which number represents the structure that produces sperm via spermatogenesis?

(A) 1

(B) 2

(C) 3

(D) 4

(E) 5

(F) 6

(G) 7

(H) 8

28. Which structure represents the prostate?

- (A) 1
- (B) 2
- (C) 3
- (D) 4
- (E) 5
- (F) 6
- (G) 7
- (H) 8

29. Which of the following numbers produces nutrient solutions called semen

- (A) 1
- (B) 2
- (C) 3
- (D) 4
- (E) none of the above

30. Which of the following numbers above represents the cowper's gland?

- (A) 1
- (B) 2
- (C) 3
- (D) 4
- (E) 5
- (F) 6
- (G) 7
- (H) 8

31. Which of the above structures represents the gland that testosterone is produced?

(A) 1

(B) 2

(C) 3

(D) 4

(E) 5

(F) 6

(G) 7

(H) 8

32. In animal's embryonic development which of the following derives from mesoderm cells, and is a flexible rod shaped body found in chordates that defines the primitive axis of the embryo?

(A) Notochord

(B) Gastrula

(C) Neural tube

(D) Morula

(E) Blastula

(F) None of the above

33. In animal's embryonic development which of the following is a solid sphere of cells?

(A) Notochord

(B) Gastrula

(C) Neural tube

(D) Morula

(E) Blastula

(F) None of the above

34. In animal's embryonic development which of the following represents a cell that is a hollowed out sphere?

(A) Notochord

(B) Gastrula

(C) Neural tube

(D) Morula

(E) Blastula

(F) None of the above

35. In animal's embryonic development the first stage in which there are three different layers of cells is

(A) Notochord

(B) Gastrula

(C) Neural tube

(D) Morula

(E) Blastula

(F) None of the above

36. In animal's embryonic development a group of cells that eventually form teeth and pigment cells in skin are called the

(A) Notochord

(B) Gastrula

(C) Neural tube

(D) Morula

(E) Blastula

ANIMAL BEHAVIOR

1. Which of the following choices describes an innate behavior that follow an unvarying pattern in which the behavior is usually carried out to completion even if the original intent cannot be fulfilled?
    (A) Imprinting
    (B) Insight
    (C) Operant conditioning
    (D) FAP (Fixed action pattern)
    (E) Associative learning

2. Which of the following choices describe an innate behavior that an animal is either born with and/or inherits?
    (A) Imprinting
    (B) Insight
    (C) Instinct
    (D) Associative learning
    (E) None of the above

3. Which of the following best describes an innate program for learning an acquired behavior in which the animal only learns the behavior if a specific stimulus is experienced
    (A) Insight
    (B) Imprinting
    (C) Habituation
    (D) Observational learning
    (E) Operant conditioning

4. The following diagram refers to which of the following pairs of terms?

   (A) imprinting and critical period
   (B) habituation and observational learning
   (C) trial and error learning and operant conditioning
   (D) associative learning and operant conditioning
   (E) none of the above

5. Which of the following are connected to the term associative learning?

   (A) Classical conditioning
   (B) Operant conditioning
   (C) Trial and error learning
   (D) Spatial learning
   (E) None of the above

6. Which of the following is another form of associative learning?

   (A) Operant conditioning
   (B) Trial and error learning
   (C) Classical conditioning
   (D) Spatial learning
   (E) Answers a & c
   (F) All of the above

7. Which of the following refers to when an animal associates attributes of a location (landmarks) with the reward it gains by being able to identify and return to the location?

   (A) Operant conditioning

(B) Trial and error learning

(C) Classical conditioning

(D) Spatial learning

(E) Answers a & c

(F) All of the above

8. Which of the following refers to when an animal learns to disregard a meaningless stimulus

(A) Observational learning

(B) Insight

(C) Habituation

(D) Classical conditioning

(E) None of the above

9. Which of the following refers to when an animal copies the behaviors of another animal without any prior positive outcome to that behavior?

(A) Observational learning

(B) Insight

(C) Habituation

(D) Classical conditioning

(E) None of the above

10. Which of the following refers to when an animal is exposed to a new situation and without any prior experience, performs a behavior that generates a positive outcome

(A) Observational learning

(B) Insight

(C) Habituation

(D) Classical conditioning

(E) None of the above

11. It is known throughout ethologists that the red belly of male stickleback fish is the stimulus for other male sticklebacks to defend their territory. Which

of the following scientists is credited with discovering that any object with a red underside initiates the same aggression in sticklebacks?

(A) Niko Tinbergen

(B) Konrad Lorenz

(C) Ivan Pavlov

(D) James Gould

(E) Jane Goodall

12. Contemporary children's cartoons depict that a newly hatched bird and a number of other animals will confuse any moving object (including another animal) as its mother. The ethologist that is credited with the discovery of this phenomenon is

(A) Nikolass Tinbergen

(B) Konrad Lorenz

(C) Ivan Pavlov

(D) James Gould

(E) Jane Goodall

13. The red underside of male stickleback fish is the stimulus for other males attacking them when they invade their territory. Which of the following ethologists discovered that these stickleback fish will attack any object with a red underside?

(A) Nikolass Tinbergen

(B) Konrad Lorenz

(C) Ivan Pavlov

(D) James Gould

(E) Jane Goodall

14. Which of the following ethologists is best known for his work with classical conditioning and the associative learning of dogs?

(A) Nikolass Tinbergen

(B) Konrad Lorenz

(C) Ivan Pavlov

(D) James Gould

(E) Jane Goodall

15. Which of the following ethologists is best known for his discovery that bees dance in a particular pattern in order to communicate the location of food?

(A) Nikolass Tinbergen

(B) Konrad Lorenz

(C) Karl Von Frisch

(D) James Gould

(E) Jane Goodall

16. Which of the following ethologists is considered the worlds leading expert on wild chimpanzee behavior?

(A) Nikolass Tinbergen

(B) Konrad Lorenz

(C) Ivan Pavlov

(D) James Gould

(E) Jane Goodall

Base the next 3 consecutive questions on the following choices. Answers can be used once, multiple times, or not at all.

(A) kinesis

(F) migration

(G) phototaxis

17. Directed movement toward light_____.

136

18. Is an undirected change in speed of an animal's movement in response to a stimulus. _____

19. Long distance seasonal movement of animals. _____

20. Chemical communication between animals of the same species occurs through the use of

(A) Hormones

(B) Pheromones

(C) Carbohydrates

(D) Answers a & b

(E) All of the above

21. Which of the following best describes the relationship between a mother bird and it's offspring?

(A) Altruism

(B) Mutualism

(C) Commensalism

(D) Parasitic

(E) None of the above

22. The handicapped hypothesis states that

(A) Animals with handicaps are less likely to survive

(B) Animals with handicaps generally don't pass their genes into the next generation

(C) Males with handicaps are attractive to females for their apparent ability to cope with them

(D) Answers a & b

(E) All of the above

23. The selfish herd theory states that
    (A) Males in a herd of their species will work to forage better than their female counter parts
    (B) Animals will stay in a herd in order to minimize the chance of predation
    (C) Some animals such as birds will parasitize other birds by laying eggs in in their nests
    (D) None of the above

24. Which of the following is not associated with mating behavior
    (A) Search image
    (B) Pheromones
    (C) Territoriality
    (D) Aggression
    (E) None of the above

25. What is the advantage of innate behaviors, compared with learned behaviors?
    (A) You can execute a critical behavior perfectly the first time.
    (B) There is no caloric cost associated with training.
    (C) There is no danger that you will lose fitness by mistake.
    (D) A desirable innate trait will be fixed more rapidly in the population.
    (E) All of the above.

26. Which of the following would not be included in an ethogram
    (A) The frequency of bears foraging
    (B) Mating behavior
    (C) When animals are out of view
    (D) Sniffing with nose elevated
    (E) None of the above

27. Which of the following is not one of Nikolass Tinbergen's four questions?

(A) What are the stimuli that produces the response?

(B) How does an animal respond to environmental cues compared with the behavior of unrelated species in the same situation?

(C) How does the behavior contribute to an individuals reproductive fitness?

(D) How does the animal's behavior develop over the animals lifetime?

(E) How the behavior came about within the species evolution?

28. A proximate cause for a behavior

(A) Is the evolutionary reason

(B) Is due to causation and ontogeny

(C) Is due to the need to forage

(D) Is due to the need to respirate

(E) None of the above

29. An ultimate cause for a behavior

(A) Is the evolutionary reason

(B) Is due to causation and ontogeny

(C) Is due to the need to forage

(D) Is due to the need to respirate

(E) None of the above

30. An individuals fitness is based on

(A) The amount of food they consume daily

(B) The number of progeny they produce

(C) How physically strong they are

(D) How many fights throughout their life time they win

(E) None of the above

31. In a diploid population how related is an individual to its first cousin?

    (A) 1/2

    (B) 1/4

    (C) 1/6

    (D) 1/8

    (E) none of the above

ECOLOGY

LEVEL 2 DIFFICULTY

Base your answer to the next 3 consecutive questions on the following diagram of a population distribution of humans.

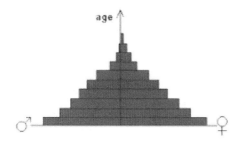

1. The above population is
   (A) Increasing
   (B) Decreasing
   (C) Remaining constant
   (D) Cannot tell from the information provided

2. Medical care within this human population must be
   (A) Rudimentary
   (B) Advanced
   (C) About average
   (D) Cannot tell from the information provided

3. The male population can best be described as
   (A) Increasing and a higher life expectancy relative to woman

(B) Decreasing and a lower life expectancy relative to woman

(C) Increasing and a lower life expectancy relative to woman

(D) Decreasing and a higher life expectancy relative to woman

(E) None of the above

4. A group of individuals who regularly interbreed, produce viable offspring, and reside in the same geographical location is best called a

(A) Community

(B) Population

(C) An ecosystem

(D) A society

(E) An ecosystem

Base your answers to the nest 3 questions on the following diagram

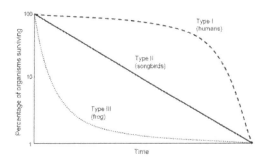

5. Which of the above curves describes a population that generally survives to middle age?

(A) Type I

(B) Type II

(C) Type III

(D) Cannont be determined from the information given

6. Which of the above curves describes a population that has a random survivorship where the likelihood of death is ultimately occurring the same regardless of age.

    (A) Type I
    (B) Type II
    (C) Type III
    (D) Cannont be determined from the information given

7. Which of the above curves describes a population that has a survivorship pattern where most individuals die young, with only a few surviving to reproductive age?

    (A) Type I
    (B) Type II
    (C) Type III
    (D) Cannont be determined from the information given

8. What is the reproductive rate for the population during a one year period if the population consists of 1000 individuals and there is 110 births and 10 deaths during this one year period?

    (A) .01/year
    (B) 50/year
    (C) .1/year
    (D) .05/year
    (E) 55/year

9. Using the information provided in the last question (#8) answer the following question. If a population were to maintain this R-value (reproductive rate) which of the following would best describe a plot of the growth of the population?

    (A) Linear growth
    (B) Logistic growth
    (C) Exponential growth
    (D) ZPG
    (E) None of the above

10. Which of the following best describes the formula for finding the reproductive rate of a population?
    (A) (Births – deaths/ the total population) x 100
    (B) (Births – deaths/ the total population)
    (C) none of the above

Base your answers to the next 6 consecutive questions on the following choices.

    (A) Mullerian mimicry
    (D) Mutualism
    (E) Commensalism
    (F) Character displacement
    (G) Batesian mimicry
    (H) Altruism

11. The unselfish relationship between two different individuals where one individual sacrifices their own fitness by dedicating time to the care of the other individual. This is often seen in mother/ offspring relationships. _____

12. a relationship between two organisms when tiny fish clean out the teeth of a shark. _____

13. The relationship between a dear and a dandelion when a dear runs by a dandelion and it's seed is dispersed to a location where there are few dandilions. _____

14. The beak size of two species of bird are unequivocally different when they inhabit the same island but when the two species exist on separate islands their beaks are more intermediate sized. _____

15. A species of butterfly that is harmless taking on the morphology of another butterfly that is poisonous when eaten. _____

16. When two or more species that are poisonous that may or may not be closely related form the same warning signals to common predators. _____

17. Pioneer species, r-selected species, and species that have efficient dispersal abilities are all

 (A) Species likely to arise in the first stages of succession
 (B) Species that arise in the later stages of succession
 (C) Species likely to arise during the same point in time as K- selected species
 (D) None of the above

18. Which of the following indicates an environment that will give rise to species that invest a significant amount of time in the development of their progeny first?

 (A) After a volcano erupts
 (B) After a forest fire
 (C) Succession on rock
 (D) Cannot be determined from the information provided

19. All of the following increase carbon emissions except

 (A) Human population growth
 (B) An increase in population of moss
 (C) Extracting timber from the rainforests
 (D) A wood burning stove
 (E) None of the above

20. Ammonification and nitrogen fixation by soil prokaryotes both

 (A) Extract toxins from plants
 (B) Produce polymers of glucose for plants
 (C) Make nitrogen available to plants
 (D) Answers a & b
 (E) All of the above

21. Over tens of thousands of years an environment transitions from dense forest to dessert. This is most likely due to
    (A) Temperature changes
    (B) Changes in average daily length of daylight
    (C) Mating season transitions for animals
    (D) Increases in carbon emissions
    (E) Cannot determine from the information provided

Refer to the following diagram to answer the next 5 consecutive questions

Algae → American flag fish→ barracuda→ shark

22. In the above food chain the producer present is the
    (A) algae
    (B) American flag fish
    (C) Barracuda
    (D) Shark

23. The herbivore present in the food chain is the
    (A) algae
    (B) American flag fish
    (C) Barracuda
    (D) Shark

24. The Tertiary consumer present in the food chain is the
    (A) algae
    (B) American flag fish
    (C) Barracuda
    (D) Shark

25. The primary consumer in the food chain is the

    (A) algae
    (B) American flag fish
    (C) Barracuda
    (D) Shark

26. In a stable environment which of the following would have the largest biomass relative to the others in the diagram?

    (A) algae
    (B) American flag fish
    (C) Barracuda
    (D) Shark

For the next 5 consecutive questions refer to the following choices.

    (A) Polyandry
    (E) Polygyny
    (F) Monogamy
    (G) Promiscuity

27. Which of the above terms means multiple males mating with a single female?_____

28. Which of the above terms means multiple females mating with one male? _____

29. Which of the above terms means males and females within a population mating with multiple mates? _____

30. Which of the above terms means one male to one female? _____

31. Bees usually have which of the above mating characteristics within their populations? _____

Base your answer to the next question on the photo seen below

32. The relationship between the wasp and a caterpillar is usually

   (A) Parasitic
   (B) Parasitoid
   (C) Predation
   (D) Mutualistic
   (E) Ammensalism

LAB REVIEW

LEVEL 2 DIFFICULTY

1. A decalcified egg is placed into a solution. Inside the egg there is 3% dissolved solutes (proteins, lipids, etc....). This egg is put into the solution that is comprised of a 1% solution of dissolved protein. Which of the following must be true?

   (A) When the egg is first placed in the solution the water potential inside the egg is negative

   (B) When the egg is first placed in the solution the solutes will start moving inside the egg

   (C) After 25 minutes the mass of the egg will be less than that of when it was first put inside the solution

   (D) After 25 minutes the mass of the egg will be greater than that of when it was first put inside the beaker

   (E) None of the above

2. All of the following statements are true except

   (A) The more H^+ contained in a solution the more acidic it is

   (B) Buffers exist in our blood

   (C) When the net movement of water exits a cell the cell is said to be hypertonic relative to its outside environment

   (D) When a cell is placed in Poland spring water the cell should gain mass after 10 minutes and possible burst

   (E) None of the above

Base your answer the next 3 consecutive questions on the following graph

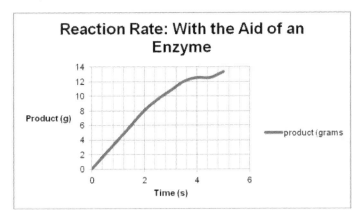

3. What is the rate of reaction between 0 and 2 seconds?

   (A) .25 g/sec
   (B) 4 g/ sec
   (C) 4.5 g/ sec
   (D) 6 g/ sec
   (E) 7.8 g/sec

4. If the enzyme were to be exposed to extremely hot temperatures which of the following would ocurr?

   (A) The reaction rate will increase
   (B) The reaction rate will decrease
   (C) The reaction rate will remain the same
   (D) The reaction will not occur
   (E) A different reaction will occur

5. Which of the following will increase the rate of reaction?

   (A) Increasing the substrate concentration

   (B) Increasing the enzyme concentration

   (C) An increase in PH

   (D) Answer a & b

   (E) All of the above

6. Ligers are a hybrid cross between a male lion and a female tiger. This hybrid causes the offspring to be exceptionally large. Some scientists even say it is the biggest cat on earth. The cross between a female lioness and a male tiger does not produce such a large animal. A ligers large size is most likely due to

   (A) Maternally inherited inhibitory genes

   (B) Paternal inhibitory genes

   (C) The lack of inhibitory genes from the male

   (D) The lack of inhibitory genes from the female

   (E) Cannot be determined

7. Substance A has high solubility and virtually no hydrogen bonding to cellulose while substance B has low solubility and strong hydrogen bonding with cellulose. Which of the following best describes the results of the paper chromatography procedure done between substance A and substance B?

   (A) Substance A and B will both travel up the chromatography paper at the same rate

   (B) Substance A will travel faster up the chromatography paper relative to substance B

   (C) Substance B will travel faster up the chromatography paper relative to substance A

   (D) Cannot be determined based on the information provided

8. Base your answer to this question on the description of substance A and B from the previous question. Which of the following explains the relationship between cellulose, both of the substances, and how far the substance will travel up the paper accurately?

   (A) Polar substances will travel slower than nonpolar substances

151

(B) Substances that have symmetrical molecules will travel faster

(C) Paper is made of cellulose and therefore substances that are polar will generate a weak intermolecular force between the molecules of cellulose and the molecules of the substance thereby increasing the friction and slowing the substance

(D) All of the above

Base the next 3 consecutive questions on the graph below.

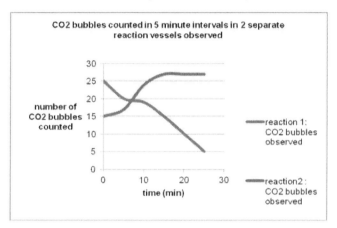

9. Which of the following would be a valid conclusion based on the data for reaction vessel 1?

(A) Plant tissue could have been used in reaction vessel 1

(B) CO_2 is being generated from the reaction in reaction vessel 1

(C) Cellular respiration was a possible reaction occurring in reaction vessel 1

(D) Primary xylem tissue could have been used in reaction vessel 1

(E) None of the above are valid conclusions

10. Which of the following is a valid conclusion based on the data for reaction vessel 2?

(A) Plant tissue was used

(B) Oxygen could have been generated from the reaction

(C) CO_2 was used

(D) Potassium Ion was produced

(E) None of the above

11. The student who obtained the data in the above graph was most likely comparing

(A) Photosynthesis in C_3 plants and C_4 plants

(B) Photosynthesis in CAM plants and C_3 plants

(C) Photosynthesis and cellular respiration

(D) Cellular respiration in a human and cellular respiration in a euglena

(E) None of the above

12. Which of the following best describes competent bacteria?

(A) Develop immunity to synthetic antibiotics

(B) Can accept foreign DNA

(C) Does not contain DNA

(D) Cannot reproduce via binary fission

(E) None of the above

13. Which of the following procedures is usually used to compare chemical properties of molecules

(A) Gel electrophoresis

(B) Paper chromatography

(C) Karyotyping

(D) Answer b & c

(E) Answer a & b

Base your answers to the next 2 questions on the image below.

14. Which of the following procedures is represented above?

    (A) Thin layer chromatography
    (B) Gas chromatography
    (C) Gel electrophoresis
    (D) Blood typing
    (E) Karyotyping

15. Staining the material in the procedure above is necessary in order to get results. The stain used in the procedure above is called

    (A) Restriction enzymes
    (B) Ethidium bromide
    (C) Ethylene glycol
    (D) Methane
    (E) Carbon dioxide

16. Which of the following would someone use the above procedure for?

    (A) Matching DNA in a crime scene to a suspected perpetrator

    (B) Comparing chemical properties between two substances such as whether the substance is polar or non polar

    (C) Mapping out all the chromosomes contained in each cell of a human

    (D) Diagnosing down syndrome

    (E) None of the above

17. A pride of lions in a particular area of Africa consist of 25 individuals. There are 13 males and 12 females. There is a trait that they all share and the break down is 60% homozygous dominant and 40 % heterozygous. The reason that there are no homozygous recessive individuals for this trait can be explained by all of the following except:

    (A) Genetic drift

    (B) A small population

    (C) Only heterozygous individuals mate

    (D) Recessive alleles are deleterious

    (E) All homozygous recessive individuals emigrated

18. Quercus alba (white oak) is a tree that occurs in many different areas of the United States. The need for water in this plant is apparent, as they grow quite large. Which of the following indicates the correct order of water potential from greatest to smallest value?

    (A) Roots, soil, air, stem, leaf

    (B) Soil, roots, stem, leaf, air

    (C) Air, leaf, stem, roots, soil

    (D) Air, leaf, stem, soil, roots

    (E) None of the above

Base the answers to the next 3 consecutive questions on the following image.

19. Which of the following procedures could this lab instrument be used for?

    (A) Separating sperm into x and y sperm in order to provide a couple with a guaranteed girl in order to avoid certain X linked genetic diseases

    (B) Mapping out chromosomes from a particular cell

    (C) Matching DNA found in a crime scene to a possible suspect

    (D) None of the above

20. The above image is called

    (A) A Gel electrophoresis apparatus

    (B) A Centrifuge

    (C) A Karyotype

    (D) Gas chromatography

    (E) None of the above

21. The above lab instrument uses viles or test tubes within the procedure. Based on this fact and your knowledge of using this instrument which of the following would be a valid number of test tubes to put in this instrument?

(A) 23

(B) 4

(C) 7

(D) 9

(E) 1

ANSWERS

CHEMISTRY

LEVEL 1 DIFFICULTY

1. ANSWER: B

DNA is held together by weak intermolecular attractions called hydrogen bonds. This occurs due to uneven electron distribution throughout parts of molecules due to a difference in electronegativity values.

2. ANSWER: C

Hydrophobic literally means water fearing and likes dissolve likes. Hydrophobic substances will not dissolve in water due to water's polarity while hydrophobic substances are non-polar (even electron distribution throughout their molecules).

3. ANSWER: A

"Hydro" literally means water and "phillic" literally means loving. This usually refers to a molecule that is also polar like water.

4. ANSWER: D

"Ose" at the end of lactose indicates that it is a carbohydrate while "ase" indicates that the molecule is usually an enzyme which is a type of protein.

5. ANSWER: E

Adenine is a type of nucleotide which is a building block to nucleic acids.

6. ANSWER: E

Histone proteins exist in chromosomes where DNA wraps around them to form a nucleosome. Histone is the only word with out the etymological suffix "ose" other than glycogen. Glycogen is a polymer of glucose that exists in animals for energy storage.

7. ANSWER: A

Electrons are shared in covalent bonds.

8. **ANSWER: A**

The first law of thermodynamics states that energy cannot be created nor destroyed. Energy can only be transformed from one form to another.

9. **ANSWER: A**

As PH increases the level of OH- increases and therefore so does the basicity.

LEVEL 2 DIFFICULTY

10. **ANSWER: E**

Phospholipids are molecules that make up a cell membrane. They have both polar and non-polar properties throughout a single molecule, hence the hydrophobic and hydrophilic properties.

11. **ANSWER: C**

The products of all endothermic processes have more potential energy than the reactants.

12. **ANSWER: D**

The rate of production of substance L would increase. All of the products will be inhibited if an allosteric effector is not used up by subsequent reactions.

Test Tip: Draw a diagram to visually represent the content in a word problem.

13. **ANSWER: G**

The rate of production of substance D would decrease AND the rate of production of substance L will decrease. All of the products will be inhibited if an allosteric effector is not used up by subsequent reactions.

Test Tip: Draw a diagram to visually represent the content in a word problem.

14. ANSWER: F

Biological catalysts are enzymes which are proteins. Proteins are made of polypeptides. Therefore, both polypeptide and enzyme are correct.

15. ANSWER: F

These are all examples of enzymes, polypeptides, and molecules that do not change throughout a chemical reaction.

Biological catalysts are enzymes. Enzymes are proteins that are made of polypeptides. Also enzymes go completely unchanged throughout a chemical reaction and a single enzyme is able to catalyze multiple reactions.

16. ANSWER: D

Substance L could be a carbohydrate, protein, or lipid. Enzymes catalyze reactions with all types of biological molecules including other proteins.

17. ANSWER: B

Glucose is a monomer of many carbohydrates.

18. ANSWER: E

Lactose is actually a dimer. Lactose is made of the two monomers glucose and galactose.

19. ANSWER: D

An endergonic reaction would show the potential energy of the reactants lower than that of the products.

20. ANSWER: A

Potential energy decreased. Refer to the Y- axis of the graph.

21. ANSWER: B

The process in the graph shows an exergonic reaction. Exergonic reactions have a –delta G. From this diagram, you can infer this by determining the heat of reaction (delta H) by taking the value of z and subtracting the potential energy value of (x + y). This generates a negative value, indicating an exothermic heat of reaction.

22. ANSWER: A

A is a molecule of glucose which is a monomer.

23. ANSWER: C

A glyosidic linkage occurs between two saccharides. A is only one monosaccharide capable of forming a glyosidic linkage, but has not already. C is a dimer of two saccharides connected by a glyosidic linkage. A polymer is three or more monomers joined together.

24. ANSWER: E

A polypeptide is a polymer of an amino acid. This piece of knowledge allows you to realize that answer E shows a repeating form of answer B.

25. ANSWER: B

B shows the basics behind amino acid structure. The R or variable group, the amine group, and the carboxyl or COOH group as well.

26. ANSWER: D

D is a lipid that is the best answer for this question. While most phospholipids are not triglycerides (lipids with three fatty acid chains), this still represents the best answer.

27. ANSWER: A AND B

Amino acids and glucose are both monomers.

28. ANSWER: D

Both the bonds within water and the overall molecule are polar. The bonds are polar because of the electronegativity difference between oxygen and hydrogen. The whole molecule is polar because electrons hang out around the oxygen atom more so than the hydrogen atoms, creating a net partial negative charge toward the oxygen atoms and a net positive charge near the two hydrogen atoms.

29. ANSWER: A

Most bonds that exist in nature are not those that occur with themselves, such as O_2; and, therefore most covalent bonds have two atoms of different electronegativity value. This in turn should key you in that most of these are in fact covalent bonds that have unequal sharing of electrons.

30. ANSWER: B

Everything in nature tends toward greater stability, lower energy, greater entropy, and greater disorder.

31. ANSWER: E

In an endothermic reaction, the products have more potential energy than the reactants; its reverse reaction would be exothermic or heat releasing. The reaction is considered an up hill reaction, and the reaction absorbs heat.

32. ANSWER: B

When an atoms gains electrons it gains more potential energy.

33. ANSWER: B

As per the PH scale and the Arrhenius definition of an acid-base, as PH increases the solution becomes more basic and therefore increases in OH- and decreases in H+.

34. ANSWER: F

Proteins are weak bases and enzymes are proteins that have subunits, called amino acids, which have amine ($-NH_2$) as a subunit to the amino acid.

35. ANSWER: C

All molecules are electrically neutral because the number of electrons always equals the number of protons and therefore cancel out. Polar molecules, however, have unequal sharing of electrons and therefore have a difference in partial charge through out the molecule. This description best matches answer choice C.

36. ANSWER: A

Lactose is made of the two monomers glucose and galactose.

Catabolic reactions are characteristic of large molecules being broken down into smaller ones such as the hydrolysis reaction illustrated in answer C.

LEVEL 3 DIFFICULTY

38. ANSWER: B

Exothermic processes usually occur spontaneously with no need for an input of energy. This occurs because the reactants seek stability and their respective products have a form such that they have a lower energy state.

39. ANSWER: C

The whole molecule is polar because electrons hang out around the oxygen atom more so than the hydrogen atoms, creating a net partial negative charge toward the oxygen atoms and a net positive charge near the two hydrogen atoms.

40. ANSWER: A

Spontaneous reactions are down hill reactions. Everything in nature tends toward greater stability, lower energy, greater entropy, and greater disorder.

41. ANSWER: C

Starch is found in plants and glycogen is found in animals. Both are polymers with monomers of alpha-glucose.

42. ANSWER: C

Excess carbohydrates undergo lipogenesis readily and easily because lipids and carbohydrates are both made of C, H, and O and only differ in their spatial arrangements of atoms.

43. ANSWER: E

The above molecule is ATP, which is used for chemical energy throughout biological organisms. ATP is in the biological class of molecules known as nucleic acids. ATP is not an energy storage molecule like lipids or carbohydrates.

CELL PARTS & PROCESSES

LEVEL 1 DIFFICULTY

1. **ANSWER: D**

   Prokaryotic cells have no membrane bound organelles and the mitochondria is a double membrane organelle involved in chemical energy production.

2. **ANSWER: C**

   While chitin is a component of fungal cell walls it is not a component of plant cell walls. Cellulose is essentially the sugar that humans do not digest and acts as a cleansing agent (fiber). Cellulose is also rigid and is what produces the loud cracking sound to a piece of celery breaking.

3. **ANSWER: A**

   Lysosomes' role in maintaining homeostasis for cells is to digest dead or damaged material.

4. **ANSWER: D**

   Cryptochromes are receptors in plant cells that are sensitive to blue light.

LEVEL 2 DIFFICULTY

5. **ANSWER: A**

   If a virus attacks a plant's cells ability to make chemical energy it is attacking its mitochondria as this is the site for chemical energy synthesis in plant cells.

6. **ANSWER: B**

   Chromosomes are X like structures that form during cell division and that exist in the nucleus of a cell and contain protein and DNA.

7. **ANSWER: D**

The fluid mosaic model depicts the cell membrane as a series of phospholipids and protein channels for understanding the structure of receptors.

8. **ANSWER: B**

Streptococcus, commonly known as "strep", is an illness caused by a spherical type of bacteria. The fact that streptococcus is a bacterial cell lets one know that it is prokaryotic and, therefore, does not contain membrane bound organelles such as the rough endoplasmic reticulum.

9. **ANSWER: C**

Many questions are developed to test the tonicity of merely the SOLUTIONS; yet, this question is designed to test whether you know the difference between hypertonic, isotonic, and hypotonic ENVIRONMENTS. The environment inside the cell portrays an internal cell environment of hypertonic and an external environment of hypotonic (which is implied since the internal environment of the cell is hypertonic). The cell will expand and possibly burst in these circumstances.

10. **ANSWER: D**

The RER does not synthesize microtubules. They do however synthesize lipids.

11. **ANSWER: A**

Describes the term osmosis.

12. **ANSWER: B**

Plasmolysis is described in this statement.

Test Tip: Identify suffixes to help define terms. In this example, plasmolysis, the suffix "lysis" means to split.

13. **ANSWER: E**

The net flow of large molecules with the aid of proteins should key you in to the fact that this is describing facilitated diffusion. The molar quantities are added as a distraction. Diffusion of large molecules will always move from high concentration to low concentration. Hence 4→ 2 Molar.

14. ANSWER: C

Blood moving throughout the circulatory system is powered by a pressure system created by the pumping of the heart. This best describes bulk flow.

15. ANSWER: G

Cellular respiration causes a build up of CO_2 in our body and since we don't reuse CO_2 like plants do in

16. ANSWER: D

Active transport goes against concentration gradients with the aid of ATP or adenosine triphosphate.

17. ANSWER: F

Hypertonic solutions cause red blood cells to shrivel due the higher percentage of water in the cell relative to its outside environment.

18. ANSWER: D

Only plant cells have a cell wall (relative to animal cells). Plant cells do have mitochondria. Animal cells can but do not always have flagella, which is used in cellular mobility.

19. ANSWER: A

Catalase is the enzyme present inside peroxisomes which breakdown hydrogen peroxide and converts it into water and oxygen.

20. ANSWER: D

The smooth endoplasmic reticulum is involved in all of the functions except protein synthesis. Protein synthesis is the function of the ribosomes which reside on the rough endoplasmic reticulum and in the cytoplasm.

21. ANSWER: C

Most of the volume of a cell is taken up by the cytoplasm, especially large cells, such as human egg cells.

22. ANSWER: C

Long finger-like projections imply a larger surface area than a smooth surface.

23. ANSWER: C

Beaker 1 has equal solute concentrations inside and outside the cell and is, therefore, in equilibrium (hence isotonic).

24. ANSWER: C

Beaker 3 portrays a hypertonic solution relative to the inside environment of the cell. This causes the cell to shrivel. Generally, this occurs in instances of hypovolemia (low blood volume) which your kidneys sense and eventually send a message to your brain, telling you to drink water.

25. ANSWER: D

In circumstances of solute concentration imbalance there is no circumstance of ALL molecules going from one area to another since molecular motion is random. The NET movement of molecules, however, can be predicted. Everything in nature tends toward lower energy, which means areas of lower molecular motion. This explains this net movement. Also the movement or diffusion of material across a membrane will cease once equilibrium is attained.

26. ANSWER: B

Beaker 2 portrays a lower solute concentration, and therefore, a higher solvent concentration relative to the interior of cells. This circumstance describes a situation where a cell may burst.

27. ANSWER: D

The golgi body package, sort and modify proteins. Think of the golgi as the UPS or FEDEX station of the cell.

28. ANSWER: E

The surface area will be too minute relative to its volume. The ratio itself will be way to small and the cell will not be able to get rid of wastes and attain nutrients at a rate that would sustain a cell that large.

29. ANSWER: C

Differential centrifugation is a method used for separating cell components.

30. ANSWER: A

A ribosome's main function is the synthesis of amino-acid chains, which form proteins. Therefore, protein synthesis would be the most affected

31. ANSWER: A

Proteins travel from the Cis face to the medial region and then to the trans face where they are released from the golgi.

32. ANSWER: E

Mitochondria contain enzymes and its own DNA, which are involved in apoptosis or programmed cell death.

33. ANSWER: D

Separating cell components is done by the procedure of differential centrifugation and alpha and beta tubulin are proteins found in microtubules.

34. ANSWER: E

The structure you should have been looking for here was flagella. Cilia has shorter hair-like projections that are involved in both cellular mobility and motility.

35. ANSWER: D

The endomembrane system consists of membrane bound organelles that work together to produce, package, and ship materials out of a cell. The endoplasmic reticulum, vacuoles/vesicles, Golgi apparatus and nuclear membrane are the integral components of this system. The ribosomes can sometimes be considered part of the endomembrane system because of their role in the production of a protein. Peroxisomes are not part of the endomembrane system as their job is to break down waste products within a cell.

36. ANSWER: A

You may be inclined to assume that the cells will expand due to osmosis; however, since the level of water intake caused the solute concentration to be lower inside red blood cells than the outside environment this actually implies that the level of water intake is relatively low and the person may not have consumed enough water throughout the day. This will cause the cells to shrivel.

37. ANSWER: F

The components of the endomembrane system include ribosomes, the SER, the RER, and the golgi. The nucleus is not considered part of the endomembrane system, however the nuclear envelope is because of its function of allowing RNA and ribosomal subunits to pass from the nucleus to the cytoplasm

38. ANSWER: A

This question tests your understanding of surface area. Smaller cells have a better surface area to volume ratio; and, therefore, the order should be smallest cell by diameter to largest cell by diameter (most efficient to least efficient).

39. ANSWER: D

Folds are a common feature seen all over biological organisms because it maximizes the surface area to volume ratio. This is why your stomach lining has microscopic folds, as it maximizes your nutrient absorption rates.

40. ANSWER: C

Smaller cells have a larger surface area to volume ratio., optimizing transport of essential material in and out of the cell.

41. ANSWER: D

Fluorescence microscopy enables you to see molecules inside a cell.

42. ANSWER: E

Electron microscopes have higher magnifications; the lenses used are much higher quality relative to the human eye and light microscopes. The wavelength of electrons enables the site of much smaller things relative to the juxtaposition in this question. Images are also seen on screens, which make the viewing of them easier for the viewer.

43. ANSWER: B

The nucleus is the location of DNA that would lead to cancer with this type of change.

CELLULAR RESPIRATION

1. ANSWER: A

Alcoholic fermentation while it does not produce nearly as much as aerobic respiration it does produce 2 molecules of ATP which is used as chemical energy for the cell.

2. ANSWER: D

Pathway 1 is glycolysis; Pathway 2 is the krebs cycle; Pathway 3 is the electron transport chain. Only the krebs cycle and the ETC (electron transport chain) exist inside the mitochondria. Furthermore the reaction only is able to go inside the mitochondria when O_2 is present.

3. ANSWER: C

The ETC is the only pathway that does not produce CO_2 because it is the only pathway that uses oxidative phosphorylation of ATP from ADP instead of substrate level phosphorylation of ATP from ADP which releases CO_2.

4. ANSWER: A

Understanding the vocabulary term glycolysis really drives this concept home. Lysis means to split and glucose is a 6-carbon sugar that is then split into two 3 carbon molecules known as pyruvate which is the reactant for pathway 2 or the krebs cycle (once it is converted into Acetyl CoA)

5. ANSWER: C

Pathway 3 or the ETC uses Oxidative phosphorylation which is more efficient than substrate level phosphorylation and 3therefore produces more ATP (36 as opposed to 2 from each pathway 1 and 2)

6. ANSWER: E

While NADH is used in the electron transport chain to help produce ATP NADPH plays a role in photosynthesis and not cellular respiration.

7. **ANSWER: D**

Substrate level phosphorylation occurs during path way 1 and 2 (glycolysis and the krebs cycle) and it produces two molecules of ATP for each pathway.

8. **ANSWER: C**

Pathway 3 is called the electron transport chain

9. **ANSWER: C**

The electron transport chain or pathway 3 yields the most ATP.

10. **ANSWER: E**

The reactants to pathway 3 are ADP, O_2, NADH, and $FADH_2$. NAD+ is used during glycolysis and the Krebs cycle.

11. **ANSWER: D**

Reactants to the krebs cycle include pyruvate and ADP but not NADH. NADH is a product and used in the ETC.

12. **ANSWER: A**

ATP or chemical energy and water are the two products of pathway 3

13. **ANSWER: A**

Oxygen is necessary for the respiration reaction to continue into the mitochondria otherwise fermentation occurs.

14. **ANSWER: C**

Oxygen is the final electron acceptor in the ETC

15. **ANSWER: C**

Pyruvate is converted into acetaldehyde and then into ethanol.

16. **ANSWER: D**

The evidence that lactic acid fermentation is occurring is very high CO_2 emissions in the form of bubbles. This process releases CO_2 and is not reused in processes like photosynthesis since it is occurring in animal cells.

Krebs cycle produces CO_2 and past a certain O_2 threshold a majority of cells mitochondria will be able to receive sufficient O_2 levels so that aerobic respiration can occur. This ultimately increases the rate of Krebs cycle activity, which will increase the rate of CO_2 released from cells. This pattern starts being visible around 5% (or just after) atmospheric O_2 levels. It was that O_2 level threshold where the O_2 to mitochondria ration was low caused the dip in CO_2 bubbles seen.

18. ANSWER: E

People who lack athletic activity will have more stored energy (glycogen) and when a certain level of stored energy is attained carbohydrates get converted into lipids, which form fat cells.

19. ANSWER: C

This graph shows that person A most likely had 3 square meals and was not relatively active through out the day. His ADP concentration would then be higher than that of person B who most likely ate 2 square meals throughout the day and also worked out twice through out the day. Person 2 would have had a higher need to phosphorylate ADP into ATP for cellular work. Also you are able to conclude that person A had 3 square meals because of the 3 spikes in glucose levels while person B had 2 spikes (hence 2 square meals).

20. ANSWER: B

Refer to answer explanation for question 19

21. ANSWER: C

You needed to realize that the slope between 15 and 17 is steeper than that of between 2 and 4. Both instances kreb cycle activity would be relatively high but between 2 and 4 the slope is less than that of between 15 and 17 (the gradient is steeper in 15 and 17).

Use the formula $(Y_2 - Y_1 / X_2 - X_1)$ to find gradient.

22. ANSWER: E

Choice A indicates that person A had 3 square meals and the evidence in this graph for that information is that of the 3 spikes in blood glucose content. Choice B is also correct because the dips in blood glucose content from the norm (which according to the data is portrayed at about 50 mg/dL) which indicates that he worked out twice through out the day. This information should key you into the fact that cellular respiration rates (both aerobic and anaerobic) are increasing. Also keep in mind that there is a clear negative feedback loop here. *A student should realize that 50 mg/dL is the homeostatic line while deviation from that can be caused by a number of factors.*

23. ANSWER: A

Lysis means to split. Glucose has a formula of $C_6H_{12}O_6$ and if you were to split the molecule you would intuitively think that it should have half the number of carbon atoms (hence 3). Glycolysis also occurs in the cytoplasm outside the mitochondria

24. ANSWER: E

The Krebs cycle is the second process out of glycolysis, Krebs cycle, and the electron transport chain. It also generates 2 molecules of ATP, occurs in the mitochondria. The Krebs cycle also generates ATP through the process of substrate level phosphorylation which produces CO_2 as a waste product.

25. ANSWER: N

A PH gradient is the same thing as a H+ and a proton gradient. These terms can be used interchangeably. A PH gradient is generated across the membrane of the mitochondria. H+ then uses it's potential energy to generate the molecular machinery in ATP synthase, which looks and acts like a motor, where it is then able to join inorganic phosphate with ADP thereby synthesizing ATP.

26. ANSWER: A

The suffix "lysis" in glycolysis means to split. Glucose has a formula of $C_6H_{12}O_6$ and if you were to split the molecule you would intuitively think that it should have half the number of carbon atoms (hence 3). Glycolysis also occurs in the cytoplasm outside the mitochondria

27. ANSWER: G

In animals lactic acid fermentation occurs without the presence of O_2

ATP synthase looks and acts a little like a motor and uses the potential energy produced by the H+ gradient to join ADP and inorganic P$_i$ to generate ATP through the process of oxidative phosphorylation.

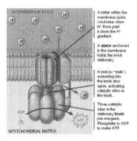

29. ANSWER: F

Single celled prokaryotic organisms do not have membrane bound organelles such as the mitochondria and therefore cannot produce ATP via aerobic respiration. The type of anaerobic respiration that they do use is alcoholic fermentation where pyruvate is eventually converted into an alcohol (ethanol).

30. ANSWER

The type of phosphorylation that generates ATP in both glycolysis and the Krebs cycle is that of substrate level phosphorylation

31. ANSWER: L

The inner membrane of the mitochondria is also known as the cristae matrix. This is the location of the electron transport chain, oxidative phosphorylation, and the H+ gradient that produces the potential energy needed to phosphorylate ADP into ATP.

32. ANSWER: C

Voltage gradients, PH gradient, H+ gradient, proton gradient, electrochemical gradient, are all interchangeable terms. These terms can be used interchangeably. A voltage gradient is generated across the membrane of the mitochondria. H+ then uses it's potential energy to generate the molecular machinery in ATP synthase, which looks and acts like a motor, where it is then able to join inorganic phosphate with ADP thereby synthesizing ATP.

33. ANSWER: J

The electron transport chain is a series of reactions that produces 34 ATP (the most efficient of the steps) by oxidative phosphorylation.

34. ANSWER: I

The only set of reactions that produces CO_2 inside the mitochondria is the Krebs cycle.

35. ANSWER: E

The highest point on the graph is a PH of 7. A PH of 7 is considered neutral. This means that there is equilibrium with respect to H+ and OH- ions.

36. ANSWER: C

The highest point on the graph is a PH of 7. A PH of 7 is considered neutral. This means that there is equilibrium with respect to H+ and OH- ions.

37. ANSWER: B

In order to answer this question you must first realize that the optimum ATP production in moles should be used as the actual yield. Since the question indicates that the actual yield is 99.9 % the difference between the actual and theoretical can be considered negligible when calculating that for every 1 mole of glucose you should yield 36 moles of ATP as per the ratio of 1 molecule to glucose yields 36 molecules of ATP. So you use this ratio to then perform the following calculation:

(1 mole glucose/36 moles of ATP) X(1.75 moles ATP) = .049 which is closest to answer B .05

38. ANSWER: E

Since the question indicates that the reactions occurred inside the mitochondria it must have occurred in a plant or an animal cell (any eukaryotic cell)

Water has a 1:1 ratio of H+ to OH- within its molecule and hence the best solvent as it indicates a neutral PH is the optimum PH for respiration to occur.

In order for a respiration reaction to enter the mitochondria oxygen must be present. Therefore the type of respiration that occurred is that of aerobic.

According to the graph low PH's which have high H+ concentrations, which inhibit ATP production.

According to the graph high PH's which have high OH- concentrations, which inhibit ATP production.

LEVEL 3 DIFFICULTY

A PH gradient is the same thing as a H+ and a proton gradient. These terms can be used interchangeably. A PH gradient is generated across the membrane of the mitochondria. H+ then uses it's potential energy to generate the molecular machinery in ATP synthase, which looks and acts like a motor, where it is then able to join inorganic phosphate with ADP thereby synthesizing ATP.

PHOTOSYNTHESIS

LEVEL 1 DIFFICULTY

1. **ANSWER: A**

   All organisms depend on the energy from the sun either directly (plants) or indirectly (organisms that depend on plants to live and provide energy for them to live)

2. **ANSWER: A**

   Chlorophyll is found in thylakoid membranes. Chlorophyll itself is a lipid.

3. **ANSWER: E**

   P700 and P680 are both identical molecules of chlorophyll but because of their interactions with different proteins their electron distribution is slightly different which causes them to absorb light at a slightly different wavelength relative to one another.

LEVEL 2 DIFFICULTY

4. **ANSWER: C**

   Carotenoids are the pigments responsible for red, yellow, and orange pigmentation. Much like chlorophyll is responsible for green pigmentation in plants

5. **ANSWER: D**

   NADPH is the molecule produced in noncyclic photophosphorylation, which is used to reduce other molecules throughout the photosynthetic process.

6. **ANSWER: A**

   Glucose and starch are higher in potential energy, which is why many texts refer to them as energy storing molecules. Starch is a polymer of glucose and 1 molecule of glucose can produce up to 36 molecules of ATP. A single molecule of NADPH can produce about 3 molecules of ATP. So in order from most potential energy to least potential energy → Starch, glucose, NADPH, ATP, ADP.

7.   **ANSWER: B**

It is the electrons that are not recycled. They in turn aid in the production of the energy rich molecule NADPH

8.   **ANSWER: B**

It is the electrons in cyclic photophosphorylation that move in a cyclic pattern throughout the reactions and aid in the production of ATP.

9.   **ANSWER: A**

Refer to image:

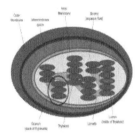

10. **ANSWER: C**

Refer to image:

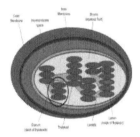

11. **ANSWER: B**

Refer to image:

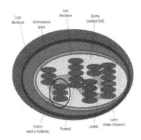

12. **ANSWER: D**

Refer to image:

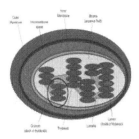

Similar to a cells cytoplasm the stroma is the fluid like substance inside the organelle (chloroplast) that is also the site of the calvin cycle.

13. **ANSWER: E**

Refer to image:

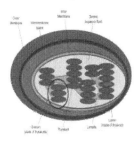

14. **ANSWER: F**

Refer to image:

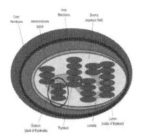

15. **ANSWER: G**

Refer to image:

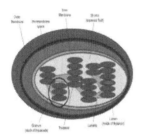

16. **ANSWER: A**

Since CO_2 is a reactant to photosynthesis and it is used, the number of CO_2 bubbles that a student observes should decrease as % O_2 levels increase. This does occur between 0-5 % atmospheric O_2 levels but then increases. The graph is actually describing what would happen to the CO_2 levels during cellular respiration at varying O_2 levels.

17. **ANSWER: A**

Since CO_2 is a reactant to photosynthesis as time goes on the number of CO_2 bubbles in solution should decrease as time goes on. Reaction 1 best exemplifies this trend.

18. ANSWER: B

The Krebs cycle is a step in cellular respiration, which produces CO_2. Reaction 2 shows a net increase in CO_2 levels which is characteristic of the Krebs cycle.

19. ANSWER: E

Cellular respiration and photosynthesis are opposite reactions where photosynthesis uses CO_2 and respiration produces CO_2:

Photosynthesis – Solar energy+ $6CO_2 + 6H_2O \rightarrow C_6H_{12}O_6 + 6O_2$

Respiration- $6O_2 + C_6H_{12}O_6 \rightarrow$ Chemical energy + $6CO_2 + 6H_2O$

20. ANSWER: B

Cyclic photophosphorylation involves the use of chemiosmosis or electron transport chain that is analogous to the electron transport chain that occurs during cellular respiration

21. ANSWER: G

Non-cyclic photophosphorylation requires electrons obtained from splitting water and stores energy obtained from light into the molecule NADPH.

22. ANSWER: A

Photorespiration not only fixes CO_2 into rubisco but also fixes O_2 into rubisco by combining with RuBP.

23. ANSWER: E

The site of the Calvin cycle or light independent reactions of photosynthesis are inside the stroma of the chloroplast.

24. ANSWER: D

C_4 photosynthetic plants transfer malate between mesophyll cells and bundle sheath cells.

25. ANSWER: D

The end result of the Calvin cycle is the energy rich molecule glucose.

26. **ANSWER: B**

The reactants for noncyclic photophosphorylation are water, solar energy, NADP+, and ADP. Glucose is produced during the light independent reactions or Calvin cycle. ATP is a product, not a reactant in non-cyclic photophosphorylation.

27. **ANSWER: A**

The products of Noncyclic photophosphorylation is ATP, NADPH, and O_2

28. **ANSWER: E**

Both ATP and NADPH are used in the Calvin cycle and also produced during noncyclic photophosphorylation.

29. **ANSWER: C**

Glucose is the final and major organic product of photosynthesis that is then used as the plants food source. It is not used by photosynthetic reactions. ATP is a molecule that often gets recycled because some reactions require energy to occur.

30. **ANSWER: C**

CO_2 is not produced by noncyclic photophosphorylation. CO_2 is obtained from the atmosphere. Plants depend on animals such as humans to produce CO_2 for this reaction process by exhaling CO_2

31. **ANSWER: B**

The Calvin cycle while light independent requires ATP and NADPH from photophosphorylation, which occurs only in the presence of light.

32. **ANSWER: D**

PEP carboxylase is only associated with the photosynthetic reactions involved in C_4 and CAM plants

33. **ANSWER: E**

In the diagram there is a H+ or hydrogen ion gradient which is considered to be the same as a voltage, electrochemical, proton, or PH gradient. Also ions are not able to pass freely across membranes in general.

34. **ANSWER: A**

The fact that both mitochondria and chloroplasts have their own DNA is evidence that they were once their own organism according to the endosymbiotic theory, which theorizes the origin of the mitochondria and chloroplast.

35. **ANSWER: B**

P700 is a pigment that absorbs light best at 700 nanometers in photosystem II.

36. **ANSWER: D**

P680 absorbs light best at 680 nanometers and functions during photosystem I

37. **ANSWER: F**

Photorespiration is not efficient because instead of fixing CO_2 alone it also fixes O_2 and the process does not produce molecules with high levels of potential energy. Products from photorespiration are broken down in the peroxisomes therefore plants spend a lot of energy cleaning up after this reaction.

38. **ANSWER: A**

Products from photorespiration are broken down in the peroxisomes therefore plants spend a lot of energy cleaning up after this reaction.

39. **ANSWER: B**

CO_2 is moved to bundle sheath cells from mesophyll cells in C_4 photosynthetic plants.

40. **ANSWER: B**

In CAM photosynthetic plants OAA is converted into malic acid where as in C_4 plants it is converted into malate.

41. **ANSWER: D**

Noncyclic photophosphorylation is NOT associated with PSI however cyclic photophosphorylation is. The answer actually describes what occurs during cyclic photophosphorylation.

42. **ANSWER: E**

In CAM photosynthetic pathways stomata are open, PEP carboxylase is active, and Malic acid accumulates in the vacuoles of the cell. Malate gets transferred from mesophyll to bundle sheath cells in C_4 photosynthetic plants.

43. **ANSWER: D**

Photosynthesis and respiration are both opposite reactions.

PHOTOSYNTHESIS – SOLAR ENERGY+ $6CO_2 + 6H_2O \rightarrow C_6H_{12}O_6 + 6O_2$

Respiration- $6O_2 + C_6H_{12}O_6 \rightarrow$ Chemical energy + $6CO_2 + 6H_2O$

CELL DIVISION

LEVEL 1 DIFFICULTY

1. **ANSWER: C**

    S phase is the phase in the cell cycle where DNA is copied by helicase enzymes unzipping the double helix and DNA polymerase comes in and synthesizes a complimentary strand

2. **ANSWER: D**

    Interphase consists of G1, S, and G2 phase. M-phase is the only aspect of the cell cycle that is not considered interphase.

3. **ANSWER: C**

    Plant cells do not have centrioles. Plant cells have a nuclear envelope that acts as a centrosome and organizes the chromosomes.

4. **ANSWER: E**

    A centromere is the structure on the chromosome that keeps the sister chromatids attached in an X like structure. The centromere is made of the protein kinetochore.

5. **ANSWER: B**

    New DNA made in S phase is regulated by the G2/ M checkpoint. While there is a checkpoint that occurs between S and G1 this is before DNA replication occurs.

6. **ANSWER: C**

    Centrioles are made primarily of microtubules

7. **ANSWER: D**

    Meiosis is the only sexually reproducing method listing while the other choices are all asexual reproduction. Crossing over occurs in prophase I of meiosis where chromosomes exchange genetic information.

187

8. **ANSWER: C**

Chromatin is DNA and protein that is in an uncondensed form. The Condensed form that the genetic material is organized into are called chromosomes. Chromosomes are X like structures highly organized by the coiling of DNA around histone proteins in units called nucleosomes.

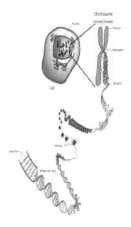

9. **ANSWER: E**

G1 and G2 are essentially growth phases. The "G" in this actually stands for the term Gap not growth even thought this is essentially what occurs in G1 and G2.

10. **ANSWER: F**

There are checkpoints after all phases of the cell cycle except for S-phase. When problems occur with the checkpoints diseases such as cancer can develop. The risk of this increase with age.

11. **ANSWER: C**

S phase is the phase in the cell cycle where DNA is copied by helicase enzymes unzipping the double helix and DNA polymerase comes in and synthesizes a complimentary strand

12. ANSWER: D

In prophase, which is part of M-phase, the genetic material condensed from chromatin into chromosomes

13. ANSWER: C

S phase is the phase in the cell cycle where DNA is copied by helicase enzymes unzipping the double helix and DNA polymerase comes in and synthesizes a complimentary strand. This portrays the concept of doubling the DNA for purposes of having enough DNA to pass on to a new cell after cell division (from $X \rightarrow 2X$)

14. ANSWER: E

Each somatic cell (body cell, which is all cells except gametes) has :

-23 sets of 2 homologous chromosomes

-46 chromosomes

-92 sister chromatids

-One X chromosome in the 23rd set of chromosomes

Homologous chromosomes are chromosomes that are the same size, shape, and they carry the same genes but with different alleles. A person gets one of each type (a maternal and a paternal homologous chromosome) from each parent.

Sister chromatids refer to either of the two identical copies (*chromatids*) formed by the replication of a single *chromosome*. In a single cell there are 46 chromosomes and each chromosome has two sister chromatids hence 92 sister chromatids present in each somatic cell.

15. ANSWER: C

Prophase is where chromosomes start to organize into chromosomes.

16. ANSWER: D

Metaphase is the phase of the cell cycle where chromosomes line up one underneath the other and spindle fibers attach to the chromosomes.

17. **ANSWER: B**

Anaphase is where chromosomes are separated into sister chromatids and pulled toward opposite poles of the cell. Each side represents a whole copy of the genetic material in mitosis and one copy will be present in the two new daughter cells produced after cytokinesis in telophase.

18. **ANSWER: A**

Telophase is the phase where cytokinesis occurs. This is where the cell's cytoplasm pinches and two new cells are formed. Each cell will have one nucleus and one complete set of genetic material.

19. **ANSWER: A**

During early telophase the nuclear envelope and nucleus start to reappear. Chromosomes start to unravel into chromatin and eventually the cell's cytoplasm pinches and two new cells are formed.

20. **ANSWER: A**

Prophase is where the nuclear envelope breaks down, centrioles move toward opposite poles, and the genetic material gets organized into their super coiled form; chromosomes.

21. **ANSWER: E**

Chromatin is the uncoiled form of the genetic material. It still consists of DNA and protein but it is not super coiled. This occurs during most of the cells life (interphase which consists of G1, S, and G2 phase).

22. **ANSWER: E**

Interphase consists of two growth phases, G1, and G2 phase.

23. **ANSWER: E**

S-phase stands for synthesis. This is the stage in the cell cycle where DNA is copied.

24. ANSWER: A

The only stage where there are two nuclei present is in telophase.

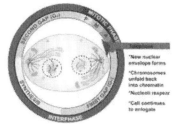

25. ANSWER: D

Metaphase is the stage in the cell cycle where chromosomes line up one underneath the other.

26. ANSWER: B

The ploidy of the cell is n=3 where there is only one set of chromosomes (you can tell this because there are no chromosomes lined up next to one another). There are also 3 chromosomes. The formula n=3 means 3 total chromosomes and a haploid cell.

27. ANSWER: E

In humans there are two types of meiotic divisions, spermatogenesis and oogenesis. Spermatogenesis is the meiotic division of somatic cells in a male into sperm cells. Oogensis is the meiotic division of somatic cells in a female into 3 polar bodies and 1 egg per meiotic division. In meiosis during prophase I there is a crossing over of the chromosomes, which exchanges or reshuffles genetic material. This is why each sperm cell is genetically different from one another even though they come from the same person (and their genes).

28. ANSWER: A

In meiosis during prophase I there is a crossing over of the chromosomes, which exchanges or reshuffles genetic material. This is why each sperm cell is genetically different from one another even though they come from the same person (and their genes).

29. ANSWER: A

All organisms that have two parents (a male and a female) have homologous chromosomes and are therefore diploid organisms.

30. ANSWER: B

Organisms that reproduce asexually will usually (some exceptions like animals that have the ability to reproduce sexually and asexually) have a haploid ploidy. This means that there is only one set of genetic information and no homologous sets of chromosomes present in such an organism's karyotype.

31. ANSWER: L

Whether mitosis is occurring in a person of a bacteria cell is always asexual reproduction of cells where the genes in the parent cell are genetically clones to the daughter cell. This is why you have new skin cells form with the exact same DNA as the rest of your skin cells (and all of your somatic cells for that matter).

32. ANSWER: H

Trisomy 21 or down syndrome occurs when nondisjunction occurs on the 21st chromosome set of a human. This causes physical abnormalities as well as intellectual disabilities and impaired cognitive function. This occurs by an extra chromosome being placed inside a sperm cell that is a homolog to the pair in the 21st set. If this were to occur on larger chromosomes in lower numbered sets the cell would die because the chromosome carries genes that are too crucial for the survival of that cell.

33. ANSWER: H

Trisomy 21 or down syndrome occurs when nondisjunction occurs on the 21st chromosome set of a human. This causes physical abnormalities as well as intellectual disabilities and impaired cognitive function. This occurs by an extra chromosome being placed inside a sperm cell that is a homolog to the pair in the 21st set. If this were to occur on larger chromosomes in lower numbered sets the cell would die because the chromosome carries genes that are too crucial for the survival of that cell.

34. ANSWER: D

Autosomes and somatic cells are interchangeable terms. These cells in humans have diploid number of sets of chromosomes while having a total number of 46 chromosomes hence 2n=46.

35. ANSWER: G

Since the function of meiosis is to half the genetic division while shuffling up your genes (during crossing over) your sex cells have not two but one set of genetic information and half the total chromosomes. n(sperm)+ n(egg) = 2n (zygote) and 23 chromosomes (sperm) +23 (chromosomes) egg= 46 chromosomes. If this is confusing think of it in terms of a math equation where you never want more than 46 chromosomes and you never want to have more than two sets of chromosomes. If this mechanism was not in place, you would end up with too much genetic information which is not a good thing. Down syndrome is the result of just one extra copy of a chromosome.

36. ANSWER: D

Autosomes and somatic cells are interchangeable terms. These cells in humans have diploid number of sets of chromosomes while having a total number of 46 chromosomes hence 2n=46.

37. ANSWER: G

Since the function of meiosis is to half the genetic division while shuffling up your genes (during crossing over) your sex cells have not two but one set of genetic information and half the total chromosomes. n(sperm)+ n(egg) = 2n (zygote) and 23 chromosomes (sperm) +23 (chromosomes) egg= 46 chromosomes. If this is confusing think of it in terms of a math equation where you never want more than 46 chromosomes and you never want to have more than two sets of chromosomes. If this mechanism was not in place, you would end up with too much genetic information which is not a good thing. Down syndrome is the result of just one extra copy of a chromosome.

38. ANSWER: J

Meiosis I is where prophase I occurs and homologs cross over and genes get reshuffled.

The function of meiosis is to half the total number of genes.

Since larger chromosomes relative to the 21st chromosome (the set where down syndrome will occur if a non disjunction event occurs) carry more genes generally the cell will just die and not have the ability to form into a viable sex cell.

LEVEL 3 DIFFICULTY

The function of meiosis is to ultimately half the genetic material in your body and produce a cell that contains your genes but still maintains the genetic integrity of a human when it is combined with its corresponding gamete during fertilization. If a somatic cell or body cell differentiates into a sperm cell in the testes they will eventually have half the number of chromosomes that the original parent cell had and therefore must be 25

If a cell has the ploidy of 2n=32 then this means there is 16 sets of 2 homologous chromosomes and therefore the organism is diploid. Gametes are sex cells that have the function of carrying a haploid or one set of genetic information to combine with another gamete to form a 2n individual. Therefore we half both the number of sets so 2n becomes n and also half the total number of chromosomes so 32 becomes 16 for a final answer of n=16

2n= 6 means that there is 3 sets of 2 homologous chromosomes. Homologous chromosomes are the same size and shape and one comes from a maternal parent while the other comes from a paternal parent. This is best illustrated by answer A because it has a cell that has 3 types of shapes (3 types of chromosomes) and 2 copies of each (homologous pair) hence 2n=6.

Since there are two chromatids/chromosome then the total number of chromatids in meiosis I would be 32 and meiosis I halves all the genetic information in the cells by dividing hence 16 chromatids present and 8 chromosomes present after meiosis I.

Molec ular Geneti cs

HEREDITY

1. ANSWER: C

C is the only choice that describes two variations of the same trait (green and brown **eye color**)

2. ANSWER: B

Down syndrome is also called trisomy-21 and occurs on the 21st chromosome set in humans where nondisjunction occurs and a 3rd chromosome is present (hence trisomy). The 21st chromosome is an autosome in that it is not a sex chromosome.

3. ANSWER: B

Huntington's disease is an autosomal dominant disorder

4. ANSWER: D

Hemophilia is an X- linked recessive disorder

5. ANSWER: D

Red green color blindness is an X-linked recessive disorder.

LEVEL 2 DIFFICULTY

6. ANSWER: E

There is a **1/12** chance that one 12-sided die will turn up a 5 and you **multiply** this times **1/12** or $(1/12)^2$ in order to obtain an answer of 1/144

7. ANSWER: A

A gene can have many variations just like ice-cream can have many flavors.

8. **ANSWER: A**

This question was designed to really test your knowledge of gametes, genetic integrity, and heredity. During meiosis there is a ½ chance that crossing over and eventual cell division will produce a gamete with each of the individuals paternal and maternal alleles for this characteristic. So since the two alleles available for the trait are (B) and (b) there is a 50: 50 chance of a gamete having either allele. Remember that a gamete can only have a single allele for a trait. Having two alleles for the same trait is acquired through the joining of egg and sperm (2n) where a gamete is only (n).

9. **ANSWER: C**

This is similar to the previous question but both paternal and maternal alleles are B so a single gamete must be B 100% of the time where 50 % of the B is from the maternal parent of the individual undergoing meiotic division and 50 % of the B gametes will be from the paternal parent of the individual undergoing meiotic division. Also keep in mind that meiosis in males and females happens in an individual. Sometimes students can lose site of this through out their studies.

10. **ANSWER: E**

During meiosis there is a ½ chance that crossing over and eventual cell division will produce a gamete with each of the individuals paternal and maternal alleles for this characteristic. So since the two alleles available for the trait are (B) and (b) there is a 50: 50 chance of a gamete having either allele. Remember that a gamete can only have a single allele for a trait. Having two alleles for the same trait is acquired through the joining of egg and sperm (2n) where a gamete is only (n). So in this case the choices test your connection to the phenotypes and genotypes as well as genetic integrity.

11. **ANSWER: J**

Two separate genes one individual is homozygous dominant for both genes and the other individual is homozygous recessive for both genes the result will be 100% heterozygous individuals or 1/1=1. You can come to this solution by multiplying the individual likeliness of obtaining heterozygous from this cross which is 1 for each gene so 1x1= 1

ANSWER: F

In this case there is a zero percent chance of obtaining individuals with short white flowers because they are also the recessive phenotype which has no chance of showing when an individual is homozygous dominant for both genes and the other individual is homozygous recessive for both genes 0x0 =0

13. ANSWER: G

This is a dihybrid cross where both individuals are heterozygous for both genes which causes a 9:3:3:1 ratio which translates into a 1/16 chance of obtaining individuals that are homozygous recessive for both genes or you could multiply the chances of obtaining homozygous recessive individuals from such a cross twice so 1/4x1/4=1/16

14. ANSWER: I

This is a dihybrid cross where both individuals are heterozygous for both genes which causes a 9:3:3:1 ratio which translates into a 9/16 chance of obtaining individuals that show the dominant phenotype for both genes

15. ANSWER: A

Homozygous dominant for height = AA and red flowers = RR. So the crossAARRxaaR'R'will elicit individuals who are all tall and pink (AaR'R')

16. ANSWER: A

The chances of getting short lillys is ½ and the chances of getting white lillys (Z'Z') is 0/0 in this cross. So .5x0=0

17. ANSWER: B

The chances of getting short lily's is ½ and the chances of getting red lillys in this scenario is also ½ so multiply the two together the get ½ x ½ = ¼

18. ANSWER: B

Realizing that the probability of getting short lily's is ½ and the probability of getting red flowers is also ½ is crucial when looking at this question. Multiply both fractions together and:

½ x ½ = ¼ or (½)² = ¼

19. ANSWER: B

Realizing that the probability of getting tall lily's is ½ and the probability of getting pink flowers is also ½ is crucial when looking at this question. Multiply both fractions together and:

½ x ½ = ¼ or (½)^2 = ¼

20. ANSWER: B

Realizing that the probability of getting short lily's is ½ and the probability of getting pink flowers is also ½ is crucial when looking at this question. Multiply both fractions together and:

½ x ½ = ¼ or (½)^2 = ¼

21. ANSWER: C

The fastest way to go about this question is multiplying each separate scenario out to get the probability so:

½ (getting Aa from a cross of AAx Aa) x ½ (getting Bb from a cross of BBxBb) x 1 (getting CC from a cross of CC x CC) x ¼ (getting dd from a cross of Dd x dd) = ½ x ½ x 1 x ¼ = 1/16

22. ANSWER: C

The fastest way to go about this question is multiplying each separate scenario out to get the probability so:

½ (getting AA from a cross of AAxAa) x ½ (getting BB from a cross of BBx Bb) x 1 (getting CC from a cross of CC x CC) x ¼ (getting DD from a cross of Dd x Dd) =

½ x ½ x 1 x ¼ = 1/16

23. ANSWER: H

Incomplete dominance is when the two dominant alleles form a heterozygote that is a blend of the two homozygous variations of the gene (i.e. red and white flowers producing pink flowers)

24. ANSWER: G

Codominance is when two dominant traits Coexist on an individual. This occurs in dogs that are black with white spots and visa versa.

25. ANSWER: K

Large spaces between loci increases the likely hood that a crossing over event will occur between them. Genes are linked when they are on the same chromosome and relatively close in distance to one another on that chromosome relative to other loci.

26. ANSWER: F

Pleiotropy is when one gene affects the phenotypes of seemingly unrelated genes

27. ANSWER: I

Epistasis is a genetic phenomenon in which one gene's expression modifies or suppresses the expression of another gene

28. ANSWER: J

Mendelian inheritance uses Punnett squares to predict genotypes and phenotypes of a particular trait.

29. ANSWER: D

Since both chromosomes carry the same genes but on different chromosomes the chromosomes must be homologous. Since the genes also exist on the same chromosomes respectively they are also linked. The degree of linkage was not discussed but the sheer fact that they are located on the same chromosome is reason enough to say they are linked.

30. ANSWER: B

The distance between A and B on chromosome II is greater than that of B and c on chromosome II. This means there is a greater chance for crossing over to occur between A and B and less likely to occur between B and c on chromosome II.

31. ANSWER: A

In x-linked recessive disorders the mother always gives male offspring the disorder because a male is comprised of an X and a Y chromosome on their 23rd set (sex chromosomes) and males always get a Y sperm from their father and an X egg from their mother. Sperm have two variations (X) and (Y) where as eggs have one (X).

32. ANSWER: C

If it was an x linked trait then an affected female would give the trait to any male offspring she had.

33. ANSWER: F

Sickle cell anemia is characterized as having an abnormality in the oxygen carrying molecule hemoglobin. This causes the cells to become shaped like a crescent moon.

34. ANSWER: G,K

Hemophilia and red-green color blindness are both x linked recessive genetic disorders. Turner syndrome while it is caused by non disjunction of the sex chromosomes it is the trisomy of that chromosome set and does not play a role in being recessive or dominant traits on the chromosomes.

35. ANSWER: H

Down syndrome is caused by autosomal nondisjunction of the 21st chromosome

36. ANSWER: G

Hemophilia causes an individual to have a decreased ability to have cuts clot effectively. This can lead to the individual bleeding out.

37. ANSWER: J

Huntington's disease usually onsets between the age of 35-44 and affects the brain.

Heterozygotes for sickle cell anemia are immune to malaria, which is why even though the disease kills before an individual is ready to reproduce the trait for sickle cell anemia lives on because of this advantage.

LEVEL 3 DIFFICULTY

39. ANSWER: D

Using Punnett square analysis of the following genotypes would lead you to an answer of ¾:

Aa x Aa= ¼ AA ;½ Aa ;1/4 aa

Notice that both AA and Aa will elicit an affected individual because the disease is **autosomal dominant**

40. ANSWER: C

Two heterozygote parents that exhibit Mendelian inheritance would produce a 25% yield of homozygous recessive individuals and a 75% yield of showing the dominant phenotype. So 10/40 white flowers in this case makes sense that the parents would be two heterozygotes Rr and Rr

41. ANSWER: F

Both crosses RRxRR and RRx Rr would produce individuals who show the dominant phenotype by a margin of 100%. Do a Punnett square analysis to find the answer.

42. ANSWER: D

This is similar to the previous question but both paternal and maternal alleles are b so a single gamete must be b 100% of the time where 50 % of the b is from the maternal parent of the individual undergoing meiotic division and 50 % of the b gametes will be from the paternal parent of the individual undergoing meiotic division. Also keep in mind that meiosis in males and females happens in an individual. Sometimes students can lose site of this through out their studies.

43. ANSWER: B

Since the genotype of this dog or the parents of this dog is unknown and not mentioned all you can conclude is that the dog has black fur based on what you see. Phenotype = physical characteristic that you can see.

44. ANSWER: E

The quickest way to get this question correct is identifying early on that it is impossible (barring things like penetrance and adhering to Mendelian inheritance patterns) to obtain Cc from a cross of CC x CC because 100% of the time according to Mendelian inheritance patterns there will be offspring with the genotype of CC and anything multiplied by 0 is in fact 0 so this must be the answer.

45. ANSWER: A

This is a scenario in which two genes and specific traits are linked. This exemplifies gene linkage where genes for different traits exist on the same chromosome and close to one another.

MOLECULAR GENETICS

1. ANSWER: D

DNA replication ensures that future generations of cells will have a full copy of the genetic instructions. Answer a and b are very similar and pertain to the above explanation. The part of the cell cycle this occurs is S- phase or synthesis phase.

2. ANSWER: D

Transcription makes a complimentary M-RNA strand in order to transport the instructions of DNA out of the nucleus and to the ribosomes, which make proteins.

3. ANSWER: B

Ribosomes make proteins by assembling amino acids from instructions that are received by M-RNA during translation.

4. ANSWER: A

Semiconservative replication occurs in the 5' to 3' direction causing there to be a leading and a lagging strand which is the modern accepted way that DNA replicates it's self. In this process each new strand would have a new strand and an old strand.

5. ANSWER: A

A plasmid is the circular DNA structure found outside the main DNA structure

6. ANSWER: E

Transformation and mutation is the only means on variation in bacteria because they reproduce asexually. Crossing over events and chaismatas only occur in sexually reproducing organisms during meiosis (gamete production).

7. ANSWER: A

Hydrogen bonds are what hold the double stranded helix shaped molecule together.

8. ANSWER: B

Ribosomes are made in part by Ribosomal RNA which contain nucleotide building blocks adenine guanine cytosine and uracil.

9. ANSWER: F

DNA ligase, primase, and DNA polymerase are all enzymes involved in DNA replication NOT protein synthesis. Helicase is used in both to unzip the double helix. RNA polymerase is used to synthesize a complementary M-RNA strand from the original DNA template in order to send instructions to the ribosome in the cytoplasm.

10. ANSWER: C

Adenosine and adenine are both nucleotides. Adenosine is one of the building blocks to ATP. ATP also contains 3 phosphate groups.

11. ANSWER: C

Smaller sections of DNA move longer distances through the dene agarose gel when exposed to an electric current for the same amount of time relative to larger sections of DNA.

12. ANSWER: A

A construction worker will build a house while a ribosome is the structure that receives information from DNA via M-RNA to build a series of amino acids into a protein.

13. ANSWER: B

The protein is what is essentially being built by the "construction worker" or ribosome. Each brick to the house is an amino acid.

14. **ANSWER: C**

The protein is what is essentially being build by the "construction worker" or ribosome. Each brick to the house is an amino acid.

15. **ANSWER: D**

The above process is DNA replication. While the unzipping of the helix can also be protein synthesis the process of the leading and lagging strand being copied is illustrated in area C and B.

16. **ANSWER: A**

Structure b is the leading strand because it is being synthesized in the same direction as the "molecular hand" helicase unzipping the helix.

17. **ANSWER: B**

In DNA replication there is always a leading and a lagging strand. The lagging strand always makes a complimentary strand of DNA in the opposite direction that helicase is acting on the DNA strand. In this diagram Helicase is occurring at site d and going right to left.

18. **ANSWER**

DNA is always copied in the 5' to 3' direction. The 5' end is defined as the 5th carbon in the sugar ring deoxyribose or ribose at it's terminus. The 3' definition is the end of the strand that has the hydroxyl group of the third carbon in the sugar ring.

19. **ANSWER: E**

Helicase is the molecular hand (enzyme) that unzips the hydrogen bonds formed between nucleotides. This is seen at site d where the two nucleotides are broken.

20. **ANSWER**

M- RNA has the function of providing the template used for sequencing amino acids into a polypeptide. T-RNA transports amino acids to their proper place on the M-RNA template

21. **ANSWER: D**

Structure 7 is attached to structure B in such a way (like the steps of a ladder) that they must represent a nucleotide. All of the other choices are also nucleotides but a complementary nucleotide is not provided which keys you in that you wouldn't be able to determine which nucleotide but you should know that it is indeed a nucleotide.

22. **ANSWER: A**

Structure A is DNA because the structure is that of double stranded and a "T" is present in one of the nucleotide spaces indicating thymine which is only present in DNA.

23. **ANSWER: B**

Structure B is M-RNA which is synthesized throughout the process of transcription which occurs in the nucleus of the cell.

24. **ANSWER: A**

This is an illustration of T-RNA. The shape and the knowledge that structure B represents M-RNA should key you in that structure C is T-RNA.

25. **ANSWER: A**

In DNA adenine is complementary to thymine. Thymine is labeled in the complimentary position relative to the box labeled 1 in structure A.

26. **ANSWER: B**

In DNA guanine is complementary to cytosine. C (for cytosine) is labeled in the complementary position relative to the box labeled 3 in structure A. This should key you in that the correct nucleotide in the adjacent box is guanine.

27. **ANSWER: D**

T-RNA transports anticodons and amino acids to the correct spot on the M-RNA template. This is depicted in figure 2 as a whole.

Uracil is complementary to adenine in RNA. Adenine is labeled in the complementary position relative to the box labeled 10 on structure C

29. ANSWER: C

In figure 2 the box labeled 8 must be cytosine because the adjacent box meant to show it's complementary base is labeled as G which stands for guanine. In RNA and DNA cytosine and guanine are complementary.

30. ANSWER: B

M-RNA is the best choice here because DNA stays in the nucleus and R-RNA is a component of ribosomes. Transfer RNA also aids in this process but M-RNA is the structure that acts as the "template delivery" man in this process.

31. ANSWER: C

Conservative replication means having the old DNA completely intact and a completely new molecule.

LEVEL 3 DIFFICULTY

32. ANSWER: E

Since the complementary strands don't match according to Chargaff's rules then we can assume that it is single stranded and since thymine is present instead of uracil we can assume that it is also DNA and not RNA. Also since this is a virus a mitochondria would not be present.

33. ANSWER: E

Mice exposed to smooth bacteria died while the ones exposed to rough bacteria survived. When heat killed S- strain and live R-strain bacteria were exposed to one another and then introduced to a mouse it died. The conclusion was that the R-strain transformed into S-strain bacteria.

34. ANSWER: B

One end of each chain carries a free phosphate group attached to the 5'-carbon atom; this is called the 5' end of the molecule. The other end has a free hydroxyl (-OH) group at the 3'-carbon and is called the 3' end of the molecule.

35. ANSWER: C

DNA is placed on the negative side of the apparatus. The weakly negatively charged molecule will be attracted to the positive end of the apparatus.

36. ANSWER: D

Transfer- RNA molecules have a 3' acceptor stem used in binding amino acids. Also due to the fact that exact base pairing in the between the 3rd nucleotide of the T-RNA anticodon and the third nucleotide of the M-RNA codon is not required sometimes there is some wobble in what kinds of codons they can base base-pair with.

37. ANSWER: A

A frame shift consists of either an addition or a deletion and in both cases will completely tarnish how the genetic code is read.

Ex: original strand-

AAT /CCT/CAT

If a single addition occurs then the code could be read like this:

TAA/TCC/TCA

Which will code for entirely different amino acids most likely.

38. ANSWER: B

This will cause a frame shift, which will completely tarnish how the genetic code is read.

Ex: original strand-

AAT /CCT/CAT

If a single addition occurs then the code could be read like this:

TAA/TCC/TCA

Which will code for entirely different amino acids most likely.

EVOLUTION

1. **ANSWER: A**

   The study of change in a population generation to generation and how new species originate from this process is microevolution

2. **ANSWER: B**

   The study of changes in groups of related species over broad periods of geologic time is characterized as macroevolution

3. **ANSWER: A**

   Use and disuse is a theory developed by Lamareck. He theorized that the reason a Giraffe grew a long neck was that they used it a lot. He ultimately believed in the inheritance of acquired characteristics.

4. **ANSWER: D**

   Traits being heritable were not one of Lamareck's postulates to his theories. All of the other listed choices (use and disuse, inheritance of acquired characteristics, and natural transformation of species) are however postulates of this theories.

5. **ANSWER: C**

   Natural transformation of species is a postulate to Lamareck's theory of evolution, use and disuse

6. **ANSWER: A**

   The interaction of UV light and oxygen formed the O-zone layer and therefore a large percentage of solar energy was absorbed by the O-zone layer so abiotic synthesis of organic molecules terminated with the rise of photosynthetic organisms because they produce oxygen

7. **ANSWER: D**

Adaptations are acquired through the machinery of natural selection. Some adaptations arise due to mutations and then these mutations (if occurring in gametes) will be passed down to a next generation if favorable but it is natural selection' machinery that allows an entire population to acquire adaptations.

8. **ANSWER: B**

A sexually reproducing organism will only pass down a mutation if it occurs in a gamete. An example could be a mole. A mole is mutated skin which will not be passed down to offspring because the function of skin cells is not to pass on the genetic code to a next generation where as a gamete does have this function

9. **ANSWER: A**

Gene flow is the transfer of alleles from one population to another.

10. **ANSWER: A**

Birds with bright coloration are usually male. This serves two sexual selective purposes. One is the handicapped principle, which states that an organism that has a handicap and remains alive is an attractive mate because regardless of selective pressures and their handicap they are still alive. The second is that many birds eat food with carotenoids and xanthophylls, which form red, orange and yellow pigments in their feathers. Birds with the brightest feathers are both able to forage most efficiently and also able to evade predators regardless of not blending into their surroundings. As a result in many bird species the males with the brightest coloration will ultimately have the best biological fitness as a result.

11. **ANSWER: C**

Use the Hardy Weinberg equation to find the answer to this question: $p^2 + 2pq + q^2 = 1$ while $p + q = 1$

For this question you must find out the percentage of $2pq$

12. ANSWER: B

Use the Hardy Weinberg equation to find the answer to this question: $p^2 + 2pq + q^2 = 1$ while $p + q = 1$

For this question you must combine the percentage of p^2 and q^2 in order to find out the % of homozygous dominant and homozygous recessive individuals

13. ANSWER: E

Use the Hardy Weinberg equation to find the answer to this question: $p^2 + 2pq + q^2 = 1$ while $p + q = 1$

For this question find the value of q from 98= 49% of population so $q^2 = .49$ from here find p from the equation given above (p+q=1) to find p and then square the value and multiply by 100 to find the percent.

14. ANSWER: E

If $p + q$ does not $= 1$ then it is said that the population is not in Hardy Weinberg equilibrium and therefore its equation cannot be applied to the population

15. ANSWER: B

Convergent evolution is not an example of what could have lead to these frequencies of characteristics because convergent evolution has to do with 2 or more unrelated organisms that develop similar traits because of similar selective pressures and niches. An example of convergent evolution is a butterfly and a bees wings (ability to fly in order to extract nectar from flowers)

16. ANSWER: E

Homologous structures are structures that have similar structure but different functions. A butterfly's wing and a birds wing would be analogous structures because they have the same function and different structures

17. ANSWER: A

Analogous structures have different structures but essentially the same or similar functions. A butterfly wing and an eagles wing have a similar function while having different structures

18. ANSWER: E

Inheritance of acquired characteristics comes from Lamareck's theory of use and disuse. This is not the commonly accepted theory of evolution (natural selection is).

19. ANSWER: E

Comparative molecular biology compares nucleotides and amino acid sequences because these are the building blocks to genes and characteristics. Lipids are essentially fats which is not a significant focus in comparative molecular biology

20. ANSWER: E

Directional selection is when an allele or characteristic has a significant advantage over another often times this causes dramatic numbers of individuals to die off that do not have such a characteristic and perpetuate those who have it. This is characteristic of antibiotic resistant bacteria.

21. ANSWER: A

Allopatric speciation is characterized by physical barriers between two populations and then the two populations diverge over time due to different selective pressures

22. ANSWER: B

Sympatric speciation is characterized by giving rise to new forms and variations within the same geographical area or within a population due to changes in selective pressures

23. ANSWER: F

When a large percentage of a population out the variation within the population often decreases significantly. Humans are said to be very genetically similar to one another because of a super volcano that erupted about 70, 000 years ago.

24. ANSWER: D

Sexual reproduction requires gamete production, which is the source of variation within sexually reproducing populations baring mutations. It is the variation

213

25. ANSWER: C

Adaptive radiation is characterized by rapid evolution of many species from a single ancestor.

26. ANSWER: C

Stanley Miller was a scientist that applied an electrical charge to a simple gas (with no oxygen present) connected to a flask of heated water. From this experiment various organic compounds formed including amino acids. This was a recreation of how organic molecules may have developed on earth.

27. ANSWER: C

The median shows growth between the original population and the population after selection occurs.

28. ANSWER: A

Stabilizing selection favor the mean relative to both extremes of a trait

29. ANSWER: D

The population after the selection event favors the lower and higher extremes for the trait. This can be seen in the solid (not the dotted graph)

30. ANSWER: B

Disruptive selection favors the two extremes of a trait. This is exemplified by the graph.

31. ANSWER: A

Genetic drift is characterized by a *random* increase or decrease of alleles.

32. ANSWER: A

Humans have pentadactyl (5 digits) limbs same as many animals. This means similar structure but different function. Ex: bat wing, whale fin, and a human hand are all homologous structures

33. ANSWER: E

Mutations are due to random chance and occasionally they perpetuate due to natural selection because they are beneficial. (keep in mind that natural selection is not a means of mutations *appearing* in populations but a means of them perpetuating)

34. ANSWER: E

Oxygen was not present in the primordial atmosphere.

35. ANSWER: D

Coevolution is characterized by predator and prey relationships where they are constantly in an arms race to out compete one another. The red queen hypothesis states that evolution can be an arms race and coevolution exemplifies this. In the book

"Now, here, you see, it takes all the running you can do, to keep in the same place. If you want to get somewhere else, you must run at least twice as fast as that!"

Alice in Wonderland·

36. ANSWER: C

Two related species or populations that have made similar evolutionary changes after divergence is characteristic of parallel evolution

37. ANSWER: B

When two unrelated species that have similar traits as a result of independently adapting to similar niches is characteristic of convergent evolution

38. ANSWER: A

Two unrelated species who become increasingly different over time is characteristic of divergent evolution

BIOLOGICAL DIVERSITY

1. ANSWER: C

There are many acronyms to remember the correct sequence of taxonomic groups. One in particular is King Phillip Came Over For Good Spaghetti (Kingdom, phylum, class, order, family, genus, species). Family is the most specific taxonomic group listed within the choices.

2. ANSWER: C

Histone proteins are found in eukaryotic cells. They are the protein in which DNA forms nucleosomes by wrapping around the histone proteins in order to eventually organize the DNA into X like structures called chromosomes. This does not occur in prokaryotic cells.

3. ANSWER: D

Another name for chemosynthetic bacteria is nitrifying bacteria because they convert nitrite (NO_2^-) to nitrate (NO_3^-)

4. ANSWER: F

Heterocysts are specialized cells that produce nitrogen fixing enzymes in cyanobacteria

5. ANSWER: B

Parasitic bacteria and most parasites usually do not kill their host.

6. ANSWER: F

Cyanobacteria are photosynthetic and one of their photosynthetic pigments they use to harness solar energy are phycoblins

7. ANSWER: C

Spirochetes are coiled bacteria that move with a corkscrew motion. Their flagella are internalized within their cell walls

8. ANSWER: A

Cyanobacteria produce nitrogen-fixing enzymes through the use of heterocyst cells. The process enables inorganic nitrogen gas to be converted into ammonia which can then be used for making amino acids

9. ANSWER: E

Nitrogen fixing bacteria have a mutualistic relationship with plants.

10. ANSWER: A

A type of photosynthetic pigment found in cyanobacteria

11. ANSWER: B

Cyanobacteria is a photosynthetic bacteria. Note: Even though cyanobacteria fix nitrogen, the group of nitrogen fixing bacteria are heterotrophs.

12. ANSWER: B

Apicomplexans are a broad category of parasitic protists. They lack motility. They are transferred from host to host by the activities of the host.

13. ANSWER: E

All of the listed choices describe fungal organisms

14. ANSWER: B

Deuterostomes have early cleavage in a straight down radial form

15. ANSWER: B

Round worms include earthworms which are not Platyhelminthes

16. ANSWER: A

Cnidarians has two germ layers the endoderm and the ectoderm. All animals with radial symmetry have two germ layers.

17. ANSWER: C

Nitrogen fixing bacteria have a mutualistic relationship with plants

18. ANSWER: C

Conidia is a structure found in fungi that carries out asexual reproduction

19. ANSWER: A

Gymnosperms are evergreens, which are not flowering plants. Angiosperms are flowering plants

20. ANSWER: B

Stamens are the male reproductive structure in flowering plants

21. ANSWER: D

The dominant generation in the life cycle of animals is that of the diploid generation because animals are sexually reproducing

22. ANSWER: D

Endosperm nourishes embryos in flowering plants (angiosperms)

23. ANSWER: A

Angiosperms produce a fruit

24. ANSWER: B

Chordates all have pharyngeal gills at some point

25. ANSWER: A

A notochord is a flexible rod-shaped body found ing the embryos of all chordates. It is derived from cells from the mesoderm and defines the primitive axis of the embryo

26. **ANSWER: D**

Rotifers are not coelomates because they have specialized cells enclosed in a *pseudocoelem*

27. **ANSWER: D**

All of the listed choices are considered part of the phyla annelida except flukes which are Platyhelminthes

28. **ANSWER: C**

Cnidarians can have both polyp and medusa stages within their life cycle.

29. **ANSWER: A**

All cnidarians have radial symmetry. Bilateral symmetry is considered more advanced as they occur in complex animals

30. **ANSWER: A**

Platyhelminthes are acoelomates because they have no body cavity

31. **ANSWER: E**

Echinoderms and chordates are both deuterostomes because deuterostomes are distinguished by their *embryonic development*; in deuterostomes, the first opening (the *blastopore*) becomes the *anus*, while in protostomes it becomes the *mouth*

PLANTS

1. **ANSWER: D**

   Xylem cells are both dead at maturity and they transport water. They lack organelles

2. **ANSWER: E**

   Dicots have:

   - two cotyledons
   - a taproot
   - 4-5 petals or multiples thereof
   - netted leaf venation

   Monocots have:

   - one cotyledon
   - a fibrous root system
   - flower parts (petals) are usually 3 or multiples thereof
   - Parallel leaf venation

3. **ANSWER: E**

   Monocots have:

   - one cotyledon
   - a fibrous root system
   - flower parts (petals) are usually 3 or multiples thereof
   - Parallel leaf venation

4. **ANSWER: C**

The statement that best describes why transpiration is both necessary and comes at a cost to the plant is:

Transpiration is a process that allows the plant to take in CO_2. This occurs by means of the guard cells opening stomata and water is lost to the environment

5. **ANSWER: B**

Vascular bundles occurring in a circle is characteristic of dicots. Monocots have scattered vascular bundles

6. **ANSWER: B**

The cortex makes up a large portion of the total volume of a root:

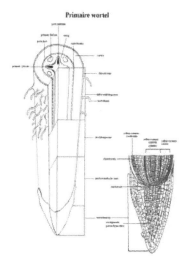

7. **ANSWER: C**

Corn will have a fibrous root system, parallel venation, and one cotyledon because it is a monocot

8. **ANSWER: A**

Phloem cells are used to transport things like sugar for the plant

9. **ANSWER: A**

Plasmodesmata functions to connect the cytoplasm of one plant cell to another so that biological material can easily be exchanged

10. **ANSWER: D**

Gibberellins are pigments meant to capture solar energy in order to generate photosynthesis. Auxin is a growth hormone in plants. Abscisic acid is a growth inhibitor. Plants also need hydrogen ion in order to grow efficiently.

11. **ANSWER: B**

Auxin is produced in the apical meristem and moves downward by active transport into the zone of elongation and generates growth by stimulating elongation

12. **ANSWER: B**

Primary growth occurs in the apical meristems

13. **ANSWER: E**

Secondary growth (width wise) occurs in lateral meristems, cork cambium, and vascular cambium

14. **ANSWER: C**

The bark of a tree is essentially its sugar transport cells. Stripping just an inch in 360 degrees could kill a tree because of a lack of nutrients being transported through out the plant

15. **ANSWER: B**

Structure A is the ovule

16. **ANSWER: A**

Structure B is the ovary

17. ANSWER: C

Structure C is the style

18. ANSWER: E

Structure D is the stigma

19. ANSWER: B

Structure E is the pistil

20. ANSWER: C

Structure F is the anther

21. ANSWER: A

Structure G is the stamen

22. ANSWER: D

Structure H is the filament

23. ANSWER: B

Structure I are the sepals

24. ANSWER: A

Structure J are the petals

25. ANSWER: B

The function of the petals is to attract pollinators with their bright colors

26. ANSWER: D

The function of the anthers is to bear the pollen which are the male gametes

27. ANSWER: E

The pistil is the female sex organ consisting of the ovule, ovary, the style, and the stigma

28. ANSWER: C

The stamen consists of the anther and the filament that supports the anther. This is the male reproductive organ.

29. ANSWER: A

Xylem consist of two types of cells vessel elements, and tracheids

30. ANSWER: A

Phloem is made of cells called sieve tube members and they are alive at maturity

31. ANSWER: E

Water is transported in a continuous stream like fashion due to waters tensile strength with originates from waters property of being a polar molecule

ANIMAL FORM AND FUNCTION

LEVEL 2 DIFFICULTY

1. **ANSWER: A**

MHC or major histocompatibility complex is the mechanism by which the immune system is able to tell ones self from non-self

2. **ANSWER: C**

Alcohol dilates blood vessels and thins blood. It also decreases body temperature

3. **ANSWER: A**

Countercurrents in nature occur when two substances travel in opposite directions. Fish have blood and water move in opposite directions in order to maximize the efficiency of diffusing O_2 into fish

4. **ANSWER: C**

In humans HCO_3 is the carbon dioxide carrying molecule in the blood. Hemoglobin is a protein with iron in the middle of it. Hemoglobin is also much more complex than HCO_3

5. **ANSWER: B**

Alveoli are structures in the respiratory system where capillaries in the circulatory system will exchange CO_2 and O_2 through the process of diffusion. CO_2 will go from capillary to alveoli and then get exhaled while O_2 will be sent from alveoli to the capillaries and eventually be taken to cells in order to generate ATP in cellular respiration

6. ANSWER: A

Alveoli are structures in the respiratory system where capillaries in the circulatory system will exchange CO_2 and O_2 through the process of diffusion. CO_2 will go from capillary to alveoli and then get exhaled while O_2 will be sent from alveoli to the capillaries and eventually be taken to cells in order to generate ATP in cellular respiration.

The Reason that there is a higher concentration of CO2 in the capillaries is that CO2 is a waste product from cellular respiration and must be expelled from the body through the process of diffusion.

The reason there is a higher concentration of O2 in your lungs and alveoli is that you have inhaled it during the process of breathing.

7. ANSWER: C

Repolarization is best described by a response to a stimulus in which gated ion channels in the membrane suddenly open and permit Na^+ on the outside to rush into the cell. As the positively charged Na^+ rush in, the charge on the cell membrane becomes depolarized, or more positive on the inside

8. ANSWER: F

The bladders function is to hold urine

9. ANSWER: A

The nephron consists of filtration tubes and is the functional unit of the kidney.

10. ANSWER: B

The kidney consists of millions of nephrons

11. ANSWER: E

The ureters empty urine from the kidneys into the bladder

12. ANSWER: C

In both males and females the urethra is the tube that expels urine from the body. In males it is located in the penis and in females it is located just above the vagina and below the glans clitoris

13. **ANSWER: D**

Urine is the name for liquid waste produced by the kidneys

14. **ANSWER: D**

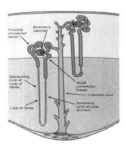

The Bowman's capsule is labeled above. It is where a nephron begins and has a bulb shaped body as seen.

15. **ANSWER: C**

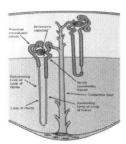

When the filtrate moves up the ascending limp of the loop of Henle it becomes more dilute due to active and passive transport of salts out of the tubule.

16. **ANSWER: E**

Urine empties out of the kidneys through the renal pelvis and then into the ureters which then pass urine into the bladder and eventually into the urethra which expels it from the body

17. ANSWER: A

The glomerulus is a dense ball of capillaries located near the Bowman's capsule

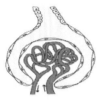

The diagram shows both the Bowman's capsule and the glomerulus. The Bowman's capsule is the "cap" on the red dense ball of capillaries and the dense ball of capillaries is called the glomerulus.

18. ANSWER: B

The collecting duct is connected to the distal convoluted tubule which eventually forms the loop of Henle

19. ANSWER: A

The contraction of the left ventricle pumps blood through the body and therefore maintains the systolic blood pressure. When the left ventricle relaxes, diastolic blood pressure is maintained by the semilunar valve in the aorta be preventing blood movement back into the ventricle

20. ANSWER: C

When the filtrate moves down the descending limb it becomes more concentrated due to passive transport of water out of it

21. ANSWER: D

The lungs do not have a capillary bed. A capillary bed is characterized by a dense network of capillaries that enables a tissue or organ to fill with blood when and if needed

22. ANSWER: B

The pancreas is concerned with the release of hormones such as insulin. The pancreas does secrete digestive enzymes but it is the enzymes that aid in digestion not the pancreas directly.

23. ANSWER: B

Pepsin is an enzyme that is found in the digestive tract. Chief cells in the stomach release pepsin.

24. ANSWER: D

Acetylcholine is a neurotransmitter that sends a chemical message to muscle tissue after an action potential occurs.

25. ANSWER: A

During hyperpolarization an excess of K^+ exits the cell causing a the membrane to be hyperpolarized (~80 millivolts)

26. ANSWER: A

If the postsynaptic neuron is inhibited only K^+ ion gates open on the postsynaptic membrane

27. ANSWER: C

Angiotensin is a peptide based hormone that is involved in manipulating blood pressure

28. ANSWER: B

Corpes becoming stiff is most directly due to no more ATP being generated

29. ANSWER: D

In the sliding filament model ATP does not cause a bridge to bind. All of the other choices are involved in the sliding filament model.

30. ANSWER: A

Cellulose is essentially fiber which is a sugar that humans cannot digest

31. **ANSWER: D**

Angiotensinogen is involved in the thirst mechanism and blood pressure.

REPRODUCTION AND DEVELOPMENT

LEVEL 2 DIFFICULTY

1. ANSWER: E

Gametogenesis is a fancy word for the production of gametes. This occurs in the testes in males and in the ovaries in females

2. ANSWER: D

Spermatogenesis is a fancy word for sperm production and this occurs in the testes

3. ANSWER: D

The epididymis is the site of sperm maturation and storage

4. ANSWER: C

The epididymis is the site of sperm maturation and storage

5. ANSWER: C

Oogenesis actually *starts* during embryonic development. The process ceases, however at prophase I. At puberty oogenesis begins again producing a secondary oocyte each month.

6. ANSWER: E

GnRH is the hormone that is released from the hypothalamus and sent to the anterior pituitary gland which in turn releases FSH which stimulates the production of the follicle

7. ANSWER: D

The hormone FSH is realeased from the anterior pituitary gland and then stimulates the production of the follicle

8. ANSWER: A

LH or luteinizing hormone (LH)

9. **ANSWER: C**

The corpus luteum releases estrogen and progesterone which stimulate the development of the endometrium (the lining of the uterus)

10. **ANSWER: A**

In males LH stimulates the release of androgens from the testes which is a broad term used to describe any steroid based hormone that functions to further develop and/ or maintain the male reproductive system. The most well known androgen is testosterone

11. **ANSWER: C**

The corpus luteum releases estrogen and progesterone which stimulate the development of the endometrium (the lining of the uterus)

12. **ANSWER: B**

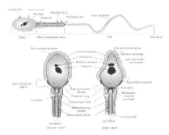

The acrosome stores enzymes used for penetrating the egg during fertilization

13. **ANSWER: A**

An oocyte needs to recognize enzymes that are released from the acrosomes of sperm cells. Enzymes are also proteins.

14. **ANSWER: A**

Human females produce 1 viable egg usually during oogenesis. Like spermatogenesis 4 cells are produced but all of the cytoplasm is transferred to just one of the 4 cells produced. The 3 cells that lack sufficient cytoplasm are called polar bodies and they die off essentially.

15. ANSWER: A

In animals the center cavity formed by gastrulation is called the archenteron

16. ANSWER: D

Reptiles and birds both have a blastula that is called a blastodisc. In reptiles and birds the yolk is very large and most of it is not involved in cleavages. Instead the cleavages occur on a flattened disc shaped region that sits on top of the yolk.

17. ANSWER: E

Amniotes have yolk sacs, chorion, amnion, and an allantois membrane.

18. ANSWER: C

Human females produce 1 viable egg usually during oogenesis. Like spermatogenesis 4 cells are produced but all of the cytoplasm is transferred to just one of the 4 cells produced. The 3 cells that lack sufficient cytoplasm are called polar bodies and they die off essentially.

19. ANSWER: A

An oocyte needs to recognize enzymes that are released from the acrosomes of sperm cells. Enzymes are also proteins.

20. ANSWER: B

Fertilization occurs in the fallopian tubes or oviduct

21. ANSWER: G

The endometrium is the inner lining of the uterus represented by letter G

22. ANSWER: F

F is the Vagina which receives the male sex organ during coitus

23. ANSWER: H

The urethra for a female is connected to the bladder and not directly part of the reproductive system. The diagram represented depicts the uterus, vagina, fallopian tubes and the ovaries.

24. ANSWER: A

Oogenesis or female gamete production occurs in the ovaries represented by letter a

25. ANSWER: G

The placenta forms from the endometrium represented by letter g

26. ANSWER: A

In chrodates the cells along the dorsal surface of the mesoderm germ layer form the notochord

27. ANSWER: H

structure 8 in the diagram represents the testes which is the site of spermatogenesis or sperm production

28. ANSWER: C

Structure 3 represents the prostate which produces the nutrient solution that combines with sperm cells called semen

29. ANSWER: C

Structure 3 represents the prostate which produces the nutrient solution that combines with sperm cells called semen

30. ANSWER: E

Structure 5 is the Cowper's gland which also produces a nutrient solution called semen

31. ANSWER: H

Testosterone is produced by structure 8 the testes

32. ANSWER: A

The notochord derives from mesoderm cells and is a flexible rod shaped body found in chordates that defines the primitive axis of the embryo

33. ANSWER: D

In animal's embryonic development a morula is a solid sphere of cells that is produced by successive cleavage divisions

34. ANSWER: E

In animal embryonic development a blastula is the structure that is a hollowed out ball or cells

35. ANSWER: B

In animal's embryonic development the gastrula is the first stage with 3 different germ layers

36. ANSWER: C

The neural tube is a group of cells that become the teeth and pigment cells in the skin

ANIMAL BEHAVIOR

1. **ANSWER: D**

    A fixed action pattern or FAP is a behavior that will be carried out until completion even if the original intent cannot be fulfilled. An example is that of male stickleback fish will attack any objects with a red underside as in the wild males have a red underside.

2. **ANSWER: C**

    Any behavior that an animal is born with is considered instinct and innate

3. **ANSWER: B**

    Imprinting is an inborn program for attaining a specific behavior only if an appropriate stimulus is experienced during a critical period.

4. **ANSWER: A**

    The cartoon is referring to the critical period, which usually starts around birth, and the first thing that an animal sees usually associates it with its parent. This best describes imprinting and the critical period

5. **ANSWER: A**

    Pavlov is a famous psychologist who worked with dogs in which they learned to salivate when they merely heard the sound of a bell because they were conditioned that it meant food was coming. Associative learning and classical conditioning is a type of associative learning

6. **ANSWER: F**

    All of the listed choices are types of associative learning

7. **ANSWER: D**

Spatial learning is when an animal associates attributes of a location (landmarks) with the reward it gains by being able to identify and return to the location.

Nikko Tinbergen observed wasps using markers (pine cones) in order to do this.

8. **ANSWER: C**

Habituation is when an animal learns to disregards a meaningless stimulus

9. **ANSWER: A**

Observational learning is when an animal copies the behaviors of another animal without any prior positive outcome to that behavior

10. **ANSWER: B**

Insight is when an animal is exposed to a new situation and without any prior experience, performs a behavior that generates a positive outcome

11. **ANSWER: A**

Niko Tinbergen discovered the FAP of male stickleback fish where they attack males because of the red underside they have. He came to this conclusion by showing that male stickleback fish will attack any object with a red underside

12. **ANSWER: B**

Konrad Lorenz is credited with the discovery of the critical period and imprinting which explain the phenomenon where an animal can mistake its mother for another animal or even object.

13. **ANSWER: A**

Niko Tinbergen discovered the FAP of male stickleback fish where they attack males because of the red underside they have. He came to this conclusion by showing that male stickleback fish will attack any object with a red underside

14. **ANSWER: C**

Pavlov is a famous psychologist who worked with dogs in which they learned to salivate when they merely heard the sound of a bell because they were conditioned that it meant food was coming. Associative learning and classical conditioning is a type of associative learning

15. **ANSWER: C**

Karl Von Frisch observed bees dancing in particular patterns in order to describe the location of food

16. **ANSWER: E**

Jane Goodall is most famous for her work with studying the behavior of chimps in what was then Tanzania.

17. **ANSWER: C**

Phototaxis is directed movement toward light

18. **ANSWER: A**

An undirected change in speed of an animal's movement in response to a stimulus is called kinesis

19. **ANSWER: B**

Migration is a large scale and long distance movement of animals. This is commonly seen in birds flying south for the winter

20. **ANSWER: B**

Pheromones are used to communicate between animals of the same species

21. **ANSWER: A**

A mother sacrificing her own time, energy, and fitness to raise and care for her young best exemplifies altruism. The relationship is a negative, positive relationship between mother and offspring respectively

22. **ANSWER: C**

The handicapped principle states that males with handicaps are attractive to females for their apparent ability to cope with them

23. **ANSWER: B**

The selfish heard theory states that Animals will stay in a herd in order to minimize the chance of predation

24. **ANSWER: A**

Search image is associated with foraging. Search image is a mental image designed to help predators search for prey

25. **ANSWER: E**

All of the listed choices describe advantages to behaviors being innate

26. **ANSWER: C**

An ethogram is a tally or frequency recording of specific behaviors.

27. **ANSWER: B**

The Question "How does an animal respond to environmental cues compared with the behavior of unrelated species in the same situation?" is not one of Nikolas Tinbergen's questions. His questions were:

- What are the stimuli that produce the response?

- How does the behavior contribute to an individual's reproductive fitness?

- How does the animal's behavior develop over the animal's lifetime?

- How the behavior came about within the species evolution?

28. **ANSWER: B**

A proximate cause for a behavior is an immediate reason or originating from causation

29. **ANSWER: A**

An ultimate cause for behavior is the evolutionary reason

30. **ANSWER: B**

An individuals fitness is based on the number of progeny they produce

You share about ½ of the genes with each of your parent and also each of your siblings so:

½ (relatedness to parent) x ½ (relatedness of that parent to sibling) x ½ (relatedness of that sibling to their offspring) = (½)^3 = 1/8 = 12.5%

ECOLOGY

LEVEL 2 DIFFICULTY

1. ANSWER: A

There is a larger population of very young individuals which should indicate that a lesser population is giving rise to a larger population.

2. ANSWER: B

Generally very young individuals and very old individuals die in 3rd world countries where medical care is less advanced. In this case there is a large portion of individuals who are young and therefore one can conclude this graph is representative of a place with advanced medical care.

3. ANSWER: C

Looking closely you can see the male side is increasing but decreasing at a faster rate than that of women as you go up the graph toward older age.

4. ANSWER: B

A group of interbreeding individuals of the same species is known as a population

5. ANSWER: A

In type I survivorship generally individuals survive to middle age and after that age mortality increases.

6. ANSWER: B

Type II survivorship describes a population that has equal chances of death from birth to death

7. ANSWER: C

Type III survivorship describes a population that is more likely to die young with only a few surviving to reproductive age

8. **ANSWER: C**

Where r = the reproductive rate r = births· deaths/ N

Where N = number of individuals

110·10=100/1000= .01/year

9. **ANSWER: C**

Exponential or geometric growth rates occur when the growth rate stays the same while the population increases

10. **ANSWER: B**

Where r = the reproductive rate r = births· deaths/ N

Where N = number of individuals

11. **ANSWER: F**

Altruism is when a mother sacrifices her own fitness for the care of her offspring. A ·,+ relationship

12. **ANSWER: B**

When both organisms benefit from their interaction they are said to be experiencing mutualism

13. **ANSWER: C**

When an organism is not effected by another organism and the other benefits from their interaction it is said to be commensalism

14. **ANSWER: D**

When two similar species niches overlap in the same geographical area often times their characteristics get significantly more different and individuals with the median of the characteristic tends to die off. This is common with finches on the islands of the Galapagos.

15. **ANSWER: E**

Batesian mimicry is when a harmless species takes on the morphology of a poisonous one

16. ANSWER: A

Mullerian mimicry is when two or more species that may or may not be closely related form the same warning signals that they are poisonous

17. ANSWER: A

R- selected species, pioneer species, and species with large dispersal abilities are likely to be the first individuals to arise during ecological succession. Examples include grasses, weeds, and nitrogen fixing bacteria.

18. ANSWER: B

A forest fire does not destroy most of the soil which enables some animals such as insects, arthropods, and eventually animals before any environment that is missing soil.

19. ANSWER: B

Moss is photosynthetic therefore it uses CO_2 and emits O_2

20. ANSWER: C

Ammonification and nitrogen fixation by soil prokaryotes makes nitrogen available to plants

21. ANSWER: D

In increase in carbon emissions means an increase in temperature and even sea levels. Carbon emissions is associated and documented throughout science to have a significant impact on environmental changes including climate change.

22. ANSWER: A

A producer is an animal that is photosynthetic and algae is photosynthetic

23. ANSWER: B

The herbivore present in this food chain is the American flag fish which eats the algae

24. ANSWER: D

The tertiary consumer is the shark because it has no natural predators and eats other predators as well as herbivores

25. ANSWER: B

The terms primary consumer and herbivore are interchangeable terms an American flag fish is both a primary consumer and an herbivore because it consumes plant life

26. ANSWER: A

Photosynthetic organisms are supposed to have the largest bio mass in stable ecosystems

27. ANSWER: A

Multiple males mating with the same female is called polyandry. This is seen in ants and bees.

28. ANSWER: B

Multiple females mating with one male is called polygyny

29. ANSWER: D

Promiscuity is characterized by males and females copulating with multiple mates

30. ANSWER: C

Monogamy is when one male and one female mate

31. ANSWER: A

Multiple males mating with the same female is called polyandry. This is seen in ants and bees.

32. ANSWER: B

A classic example of a parasitoid is the wasp laying her eggs inside a caterpillar and the caterpillar nourishes the eggs by consuming nutrients and eventually the eggs hatch and kill the caterpillar.

LAB REVIEW

LEVEL 2 DIFFICULTY

1. **ANSWER: D**

   The solution outside the decalcified egg is hypotonic and water always has a net movement of hypotonic solutions to hypertonic solutions through a semipermeable membrane

2. **ANSWER: C**

   When the net movement of water exits a cell, the cells environment must have a lower solute concentration relative to the outside environment and therefore be hypotonic relative to the outside environment.

3. **ANSWER: B**

   Use the formula $y_2\text{-}y_1/x_2\text{-}x_1$

   So $8\text{-}0/2\text{-}0 = 4$ g/second

4. **ANSWER: B**

   All proteins including enzymes are sensitive to sharp temperature and PH fluctuations. Deviation from dynamic equilibrium will change the shape of the enzyme, which renders it useless. An enzymes function is to catalyze reactions, which make them occur faster. This means the reaction will still occur but they will do so much slower.

5. **ANSWER: D**

   An increase in the enzyme concentration or substrate concentration will make the reaction occur faster.

6. **ANSWER: D**

   Female lions have inhibitory genes for lions while males have genes to make them larger. When a male lion and a female tiger mate there are no inhibitory genes that are present in the joining of both genetic materials so a very large cat is produced.

7. **ANSWER: B**

   Low solubility and hydrogen bonding with cellulose will cause more friction which will cause the substance to travel slower up the chromatograph

8. **ANSWER: D**

   Low solubility and hydrogen bonding with cellulose will cause more friction which will cause the substance to travel slower up the chromatograph

9. **ANSWER: A**

   Reaction 1 shows a decrease in CO_2, which indicates that CO_2 is being used. Photosynthesis uses CO_2 which is a process that occurs in plant tissue

10. **ANSWER: E**

    Reaction 2 is most likely a cellular respiration reaction because it produces CO_2. The choices all indicate characteristics of photosynthesis occurring with the exception of answer choice D which does not belong in either process

11. **ANSWER: C**

    The trends between reaction vessel 1 and 2 indicate trends seen when comparing photosynthesis and respiration (opposite reactions).

    Photosynthesis uses CO_2 while cellular respiration produces CO_2

12. **ANSWER: B**

    Competent bacteria has the ability to accept foreign DNA

13. **ANSWER: B**

    Gel electrophoresis looks at the size of DNA molecules which is a physical property of a molecule while paper chromatography looks at solubility and polarity which are chemical properties

14. **ANSWER: C**

    Gel electrophoresis is represented in the image above

15. **ANSWER: B**

Ethidium bromide is used to stain DNA so that it can be seen under a black light. Ethidium bromide is also a mutagen.

16. **ANSWER: A**

Gel electrophoresis is a procedure that is used in determining DNA matches in paternity testing and crime scene investigating

17. **ANSWER: C**

Heterozygous individuals mating would lead to some homozygous dominant individuals being born as long as they are mating with other heterozygotes within the population

18. **ANSWER: B**

Water potential is highest in the soil then, the roots, shoots, stems, and then leaves have the lowest water potential

19. **ANSWER: A**

The image represents a centrifuge, which can be used to separate things that are different sizes and densities such as X, and Y sperm cells.

20. **ANSWER: B**

The image represents a centrifuge, which can be used to separate things that are different sizes and densities such as X, and Y sperm cells.

21. **ANSWER: B**

In a centrifuge there must be an even number of viles each weighing the same in order to safely balance the centrifuge

Made in the USA
Middletown, DE
12 January 2019